D0065754

GAYLE E. PITMAN
FOREWORD BY FRED SARGEANT

THE STONEWALL RIOTS

Coming Out
in the Streets

**ABRAMS BOOKS
FOR YOUNG READERS**

NEW YORK

Cataloging-in-Publication Data has been applied for
and may be obtained from the Library of Congress.

ISBN 978-1-4197-3720-6

Text copyright © 2019 Gayle E. Pitman

Book design by Sara Corbett

For image credits, see page 192.

Printed and bound in U.S.A.
10 9 8 7 6 5 4 3 2 1

Abrams Books for Young Readers are available at special discounts
when purchased in quantity for premiums and promotions as well as
fundraising or educational use. Special editions can also be created to specification.
For details, contact specialsales@abramsbooks.com or the address below.

ABRAMS The Art of Books
195 Broadway, New York, NY 10007
abramsbooks.com

CONTENTS

AFTERMATH 103

LIBERATION 123

FOREWORD

Although I'd known years earlier that I was different from friends, it wasn't until I was thirteen that I realized the difference was that I was gay. No one else knew. I didn't know others who might be gay and did what was common among young gays in the 1960s: As soon as I could, I moved to Greenwich Village in New York City. I was nineteen. Soon after getting there, I met a young gay activist, Craig Rodwell, and we became partners. Craig's commitment to truth captured my attention. He was a true pioneer for his time.

Craig introduced me to so many of the people in the story that follows, and it's been my privilege to share my recollections with its author, Gayle Pitman. Gayle has always been a strong listener for the everyday aspects of a story and communicates that well in her narrative.

Over the past fifty years, we have gone from the age of orderly boy-and-girl picketing—a picket that was single file or male-female couples only to present a nonthreatening image for straight people—to utilizing the centuries-old tool of leafletting, to an age of texts and social media. But in the 1950s, '60s, and '70s, leaflets abounded and carried the same clues to commerce and politics in a community that texts and social media do today. Leaflets produced what back then passed for immediate results! The morning after the Stonewall Riots, we handed out leaflets in the West Village, calling for further demonstrations by young people in the area that evening to protest the corrupt ties between the mob–gay bar syndicate and the New York police department. It was the immediacy with passersby on the street while leafletting that produced the second night's crowds at Stonewall.

The late 1960s became a period of explosive political expansion by the LGBT community, with LGBT youth at the forefront of it. Gayle's work captures this tumultuous time and accurately reports on the fact-shy myths that have grown up around Stonewall and Pride.

If life can be said to be an accumulation of experiences that guide our decisions, then in my case, it may certainly be said that the experiences of those nights at Stonewall, and then Pride, led to a career in policing and further activism. The many others involved with Stonewall and Pride became academics, entertainers, writers, engineers, and business leaders. We were all forever changed by the experience of Stonewall, and later Pride. And we are all the better for it. —*Fred Sargeant*

FRED SARGEANT was at the front line of the LGBT movement and was actively involved in the Stonewall Riots and in the emergence of Pride. Today he is a retired lieutenant from the Stamford, Connecticut, police department.

INTRODUCTION

> "Every object tells a story
> if you know how to read it."
> —HENRY FORD

O bjects can tell the story of a person's life. And they can tell a lot about an event, a period in history, or a moment in time. Studying objects and the stories they tell about history and culture involves what's called "material culture." Museums are filled with exhibits involving material culture. Objects might include tools, items of clothing, newspaper articles, letters, jewelry, or other personal items. They could include public objects, such as street signs, billboards, playground equipment, or other items in common spaces. Most of these items might seem mundane and boring—but when put together, those objects can tell a very interesting story.

Using objects to understand history is a particularly good way to tell a story that's complicated—especially if that story differs depending on who tells it. Telling a story through objects is like viewing something through a kaleidoscope. Each fragment seems entirely separate, but together they form a colorful, multifaceted image. What happens when the tube turns? The image changes! And while the new image is still made up of the original fragments, it's impossible to reconstruct the image viewed before that. That's what the history of the Stonewall Riots is like. It's a complex story, made up of many fragments and dimensions, and it's a challenging history to reconstruct.

What *really* happened in the early morning hours of June 28, 1969? It was chaotic, and the riots lasted for several days. Some people said they were there, and there is evidence to support that. Others claim to have been there, but that evidence is more murky. There are arguments about who started the riots and what the exact sequence of events were. The people who were part of this complicated story include seemingly unrelated groups of people, including gay men, lesbian women, cross-dressers and drag queens,

---

In the 1960s, the terms, *queen*, *drag queen*, and *transvestite* were used interchangeably to describe men who dressed in women's clothing, or who identified as women. The term *transgender* was not commonly used during that time period. Today transgender refers to people whose sense of personal identity and gender does not correspond with their birth sex.

---

homeless street kids, the Mafia, the police, and the residents of Greenwich Village. While many of their stories overlap, none of their stories are exactly the same.

Choosing objects for this book is like curating a museum exhibition. People who work in museums have to determine which items are important in telling a story, and which items are not. It's a challenging task, and it involves making hard decisions. Many of the objects chosen for this book are authentic and are still in existence. Other objects are examples or replicas of what would have existed at the time. Because this is a history of a series of riots and uprisings, a lot of objects were destroyed and are no longer available. But in order to tell this story accurately, it's important to include them all.

BEFORE THE RIOTS

Greenwich Village is one of the most vibrant and bustling neighborhoods in New York City, filled with apartment buildings, brownstone row houses, shops, and restaurants. It's also one of the most famous gay neighborhoods in the world. If you visit Greenwich Village today, you'll probably see rainbow flags flying from apartment balconies, same-sex couples holding hands as they walk down the street together, and flyers advertising LGBTQ+ events. (The terms *LGBT* and *LGBTQ+* have evolved over time. Around the time of the Stonewall Riots, the terms *gay* and *lesbian* were the primary way to refer to this community. Later *B*—for bisexual—was added, and then *T*—for transgender—was included. More recently, the *Q+* was added to include individuals who identify with "queer" or "questioning." These additions occurred after the riots, so throughout the manuscript, for simplicity, LGBT is used, unless referring to contemporary times.)

However, Greenwich Village wasn't always this way. Back in the 1600s, the Village was more country than city, with tobacco farms dotting the landscape. In the 1700s, when malaria, yellow fever, and cholera outbreaks hit the southern tip of New York City (which today is the financial district of Manhattan), people who had money fled north to the small countryside "village of Greenwich," seeking fresh air and a rural atmosphere. By the mid-1800s, Greenwich Village was a well-established neighborhood, the streets lit by gas lamps and dotted with horse stables. The mazelike, crooked paths that were originally worn down by foot traffic and horse-drawn carriages is the same footprint we see in today's paved Greenwich Village roadways.

Greenwich Village has been a center of the LGBT community since the late 1800s. The Black Rabbit, located at 183 Bleecker Street, and the Slide (otherwise known as the Fairy Resort), at 157 MacDougal Street, were the first places in New York City where gay people could socialize. Through the first half of the 1900s, being openly gay was very dangerous. Bars and clubs were regularly raided by the police, and the gay bar patrons were routinely arrested, sent to psychiatric wards for treatment, and generally rejected by mainstream society.

These first objects will give you a sense of what it was like to be gay back in the late 1800s and early 1900s. You'll also see what the site of the Stonewall Inn looked like more than a hundred years ago, and how it evolved into what it is today.

JEFFERSON LIVERY STABLES

I n New York City in the 1840s, there were no buses or subways. There were no Yellow Cabs or honking horns. There were, however, plenty of footpaths, dirt roads, horse-drawn carriages, and, of course, horses. The horses had to live somewhere, and that's where the story of the Stonewall Inn begins.

The Stonewall Inn is located at 51 and 53 Christopher Street in Greenwich Village. The buildings that now house the Stonewall Inn were both built in the 1840s—for horses, not for people! In 1843, the first of two livery stables was built at the 51 site, and the stable at 53 was built in 1846. At that time, between one and two hundred thousand horses lived in New York City—enough to fill a midsize city! Throughout the 1800s, New York City was also home to sheep, cows, pigs, and other farm animals, and sounders of pigs commonly roamed the streets. (A group of pigs is called a "sounder.") By the late 1800s, there were so many horses and other animals in the city that it was causing a public health nuisance. Manure piles filled the streets, attracting flies. Horse carcasses were left on the streets to rot. Can you imagine what the city must have smelled like?

Public health issues aside, the horses that lived at the Jefferson Livery Stables had a very important job. They were responsible for delivering the finest men's and women's fashions to the exclusive Saks & Company store on 34th Street. Every day, the horses were groomed until their black coats shone, and their hooves were painted black and polished like patent leather shoes. Saks & Company was one of the most elite stores in New York City, and the horses that delivered the goods were a reflection of Saks's high-class image.

MATCHBOOK, BONNIE'S STONEWALL INN

By the 1930s, cars were much more common than horses in American cities, and horse-drawn carriages were quickly being phased out. Livery stables began to close, and many of the buildings that housed the stables—including the Jefferson Livery Stables—were converted into commercial business spaces. The space reopened in 1930 as Bonnie's Stone Wall, a tearoom that also operated as a speakeasy—a place that served alcohol illegally during Prohibition. From 1920 to 1933, Prohibition laws had banned the production, sale, and consumption of alcohol. In 1934, shortly after Prohibition laws were repealed, Bonnie's Stone Wall became a more legitimate operation. As time passed, the name changed to Bonnie's Stonewall Inn, a respectable cocktail bar and restaurant that was known for hosting weddings, parties, and banquets.

Where did the name Stonewall come from? There's no definitive answer to that question. It's possible that the inspiration came from a book published in 1930 titled *The Stone Wall*. Written by Ruth Fuller Field under the pen name Mary Casal, *The Stone Wall* was an autobiographical account of her romantic relationship with another woman. The name Stone Wall may have been a way to send a coded welcome message to lesbians.

TRIAL TRANSCRIPT, JUNE 8, 1903

Throughout the early 1900s, homosexual subculture had a growing presence in most major cities, including New York, San Francisco, Chicago, and Los Angeles. People who experience discrimination, mistreatment, and persecution often try to create safe spaces where they can gather and socialize with one another. That was especially true for gay and lesbian people, who couldn't easily identify one another based on their appearance, and who needed to keep their identities under wraps in order to avoid arrest or public humiliation. As a result, bars and social clubs that catered to gay and lesbian people began to pop up in major cities across the United States. Most of these establishments were located in basements and back rooms of hotels and restaurants—places that wouldn't be easily detectable to the police.

Unfortunately, the rise of homosexual subcultures also intensified the activities of police morals and vice squads.

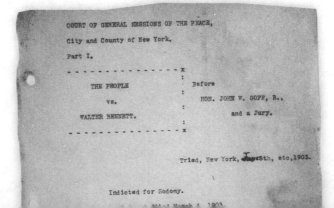

COURT OF GENERAL SESSIONS OF THE PEACE,
City and County of New York.
Part I.
- - - - - - - - - - - - - - - - - x
           :
  THE PEOPLE   :   Before
           :
     vs.   :   HON. JOHN W. GOFF, R.,
           :   and a Jury.
  WALTER BENNETT. :
- - - - - - - - - - - - - - - - - x

Tried, New York, June 8th, etc, 1903.

Indicted for Sodomy.

These departments were responsible for ridding their cities of immoral behaviors such as gambling, public intoxication, prostitution, or other acts considered to be corrupt, deviant, or otherwise socially unacceptable—including homosexuality.

February 21, 1903, was the first documented police raid of a gay establishment in the United States. Police raided the basement of the Ariston Hotel in New York City, located on the corner of 55th Street and Broadway, where gay men were suspected of socializing. The manager of this space was rumored to be gay, and the police had been keeping their eye on the Ariston for some time. Fourteen men were arrested, and sixty more were detained by the police. Even worse, the names and home addresses of some of the men were printed in the morning newspapers. The threat of being outed (having your sexuality revealed to the public) was enough to keep most gay men in the closet, and the police viewed public humiliation as a powerful deterrent to homosexual behavior. For the next few decades, police raids became increasingly common, and stories about police raids of gay establishments—sometimes written in highly sensationalistic ways—began to appear in urban newspapers throughout the United States.

Some of the men who were arrested were charged with

disorderly conduct or for violating liquor laws. Others were charged with sodomy—having sex with another man—and most of those cases were sent to trial. The lawyers who represented the men on trial used a variety of tactics to defend their innocence, particularly for men who were high-class, well-respected members of the community. One attorney showed off his client's engagement ring to prove he was heterosexual. Another called a series of character witnesses to the stand, including a minister and a woman with whom his client had been romantically involved, to prove that his client was a Bible-following, heterosexual man. Still another argued that his client was a "real man" because he fought against the police during his arrest. In the end, while only a few men were ultimately found guilty, all of them experienced public humiliation.

Sometimes the morals and vice squads would use entrapment tactics in order to catch unsuspecting gay men—which is what happened in 1918 at the Baker Street Club in San Francisco, a private residence that had been converted into a social space. Concerned that gay men were members of the Baker Street Club, the morals squad sent an undercover officer to pose as a cook, apply for a job at the club, and spy on the people inside. On February 16, 1918, police surrounded and raided the building, then spent the next ten days locking patrons in rooms, interrogating them, and forcing them to sign confessions. This sting operation led to the arrest of at least thirty-one men, and the information gathered at the Baker Street raid led to a wider investigation of homosexuality in other cities. The message was clear from these raids: Homosexuality was considered to be criminal behavior, and people could be arrested and jailed for it.

Most newspaper articles published in the early 1900s didn't use the words "gay" or "homosexual" and they didn't mention specific behaviors. Instead, we see phrases like "scores of men in various walks of life" (which is code for gay). This was common in newspapers at the time. In one article published by the *San Francisco Chronicle*, a club that was raided was described as "a rendezvous for a large number of vicious men." There were at least two reasons for this. First, people didn't use the words "gay" and "homosexual" in the early 1900s, so it makes sense that we wouldn't see those terms in a newspaper article written during that time period. But the other reason was more of a moralistic one—reporters who wrote for reputable newspapers were forbidden to use language that was considered to be profane or obscene, and anything associated with homosexuality fell into that category.

1950s
TELEVISION

During World War II, thousands of U.S. soldiers were overseas fighting, and there weren't enough men to keep the factories, mines, and other industries open and in business. Guess who came to the rescue? Women! The U.S. government started a nationwide campaign to entice women to leave their traditional roles of housewives and mothers and join the traditionally male workforce as part of the war effort. Rosie the Riveter, with her red bandanna and flexed biceps, became a symbol of patriotism and an iconic image of the 1940s. It was a time when gender roles were being challenged, because the United States needed all hands on deck in order to keep the country's economy up and running.

When the war ended, all of that changed. Men came home from the war, and women were thanked for their service and told to go back to being housewives. But some women didn't want to do that. They liked being in the workforce. Learning new skills, meeting people, and earning money gave them a sense of power and independence.

Television became a means to help reinforce women's roles as housewives and stay-at-home moms. Most TV shows

in the 1950s featured white, middle-class, traditional nuclear families, complete with a dad who went off to work every day in a suit, a mom who wore a housedress and smiled while she vacuumed and dusted, and ragamuffin kids who were always getting into mischief. During commercial breaks, ads showcased colorful new kitchen appliances (to keep women in the kitchen) and TV dinners (to keep families in front of the television). On top of that, the government passed laws establishing morality codes, which made clear what kinds of content could be shown on television, and what kind could not. All of these were powerful tactics of persuasion, designed to promote a sense of traditionalism and "family values."

What does all of this have to do with the Stonewall Riots? Quite a bit, actually. Television shows in the 1950s made life look rosy and fun—at least if you were white, middle-class, and heterosexual. In contrast, the climate for gay and lesbian people during that time period was very threatening—and at that time, this reality was *never* shown on television. The end of World War II gave rise to a widespread fear of communism in the United States, also known as the Red Scare. Anyone who was considered to be different, radical, leftist, antiestablishment, or nontraditional in any way was at risk for being labeled a communist, including people who were gay. As a result, the social consequences of being gay escalated sharply during the 1950s. Gay people (or people who were merely suspected of being gay) could be arrested and jailed, just as they had been for decades. Or they could be diagnosed by a psychologist or psychiatrist with homosexuality (which was considered to be a mental illness at the time) and sent to a psychiatric hospital. They could be fired from their jobs, and they could lose their housing. Their names and addresses could be made public, and they could be labeled as homosexuals and as communists. It was a terrifying time to be gay, for sure. And not surprisingly, police raids of gay bars, clubs, and social establishments increased. The only media coverage about gay people involved news articles about these raids. In these articles, journalists shifted away from using modest and veiled language, and instead described gay people in insulting and derogatory ways. They described in lurid detail the scandal and immorality of homosexuality. These articles were designed to keep gay men and lesbians in the closet, and it worked—at least for a little while.

PHOTOGRAPH, MATTACHINE SOCIETY MEETING

(UPPER LEFT) Harry Hay; (LEFT TO RIGHT) Konrad Stevens, Dale Jennings, Rudi Gernreich, Stan Witt, Bob Hull, Chuck Rowland (WEARING GLASSES), Paul Bernard

I t was 1950, and negative attitudes against homosexuals were quickly reaching a saturation point. Many gay and lesbian people began to believe the anti-gay propaganda— that they were sick and immoral people who engaged in repulsive behaviors. But there were a few people who knew that these were all lies, and they were ready to take action. They also knew this: You need an organized community if you want to create change. And you can't create change if you can't find each other. Since so many gay and lesbian people kept their identities secret, finding each other was going to be a challenge.

Harry Hay was ready to take on that challenge. Harry got his start in the 1930s labor movement, advocating for safe working conditions, fair pay, and reasonable work hours. Later, he became a member of the Communist Party, which, in mainstream society, was considered to be anti-American. At the time, the Party was working for all the things he believed in, such as antidiscrimination laws in the workplace and guaranteed medical care. For Harry, working with the Party was kind of like going to activist school—it taught him everything he needed to know about starting an underground organization. So in 1950, when fear of gay people was escalating, Harry and his friends Rudi Gernreich, Chuck Rowland, Bob Hull, and Dale Jennings gathered in his living room in Los Angeles to plot a gay revolution—and that's how the Mattachine Society came to be. The Mattachine Society was the first homophile (meaning same-love) organization in the United States, and it marked the launch of a larger homophile movement.

What exactly does the word "Mattachine" mean? Harry and his friends were inspired by the medieval Italian *mattachinos*, troupes of truth-telling court jesters who traveled from village to village, conveying their message through songs and performances. While the Mattachine Society refrained from singing and dancing, the founding members believed strongly that their mission was to tell the truth about gay people, and to celebrate their existence.

As the Red Scare escalated during the 1950s, the Mattachine Society decided to protect its members by detaching itself from communism. At that point, the group became more conventional and conformist. Members were discouraged from using their real names on membership lists so they wouldn't be identified by the government. Moreover, they were expected to dress and act conservatively, with short hair, jackets and ties, and restrained behavior—the idea being that mainstream society might be more likely to accept them if they behaved well. In May of 1953, because the group was moving in a more conservative direction, all of the original members resigned, including Harry Hay.

DAUGHTERS OF BILITIS STATEMENT OF PURPOSE

I n many ways, Del Martin and Phyllis Lyon are a classic lesbian love story. They met in 1950, became a couple in 1952, and bought a house and moved in together on Valentine's Day, February 14, 1955. They were active in their community, and they remained together for fifty-six years, until Del passed away on August 27, 2008.

Here's the catch: It was the 1950s, and it wasn't safe for people to be openly gay or lesbian. Del and Phyllis felt isolated and had a hard time finding lesbian friends. A gay male couple they knew introduced them to another lesbian couple, and together they started a social club. The first meeting of the Daughters of Bilitis (DOB) was in October of 1955. Initially, they wanted a social outlet and a place to dance (because it was illegal for a woman to dance with another woman, or a man to dance with another man, in a public place). However, it quickly became clear that the group needed to be more organized, and they elected Del Martin as president. They decided to focus their efforts on educating others about lesbians, as well as promoting self-acceptance. The name of the group was inspired by *The Songs of Bilitis*, a collection of lesbian poetry by a French writer named Pierre

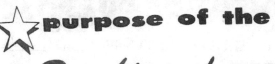

purpose of the
Daughters of BILITIS

A WOMEN'S ORGANIZATION FOR THE PURPOSE OF PROMOTING
THE INTEGRATION OF THE HOMOSEXUAL INTO SOCIETY BY:

1 Education of the variant, with particular emphasis on the psychological, physiological and sociological aspects, to enable her to understand herself and make her adjustment to society in all its social, civic and economic implications——this to be accomplished by establishing and maintaining as complete a library as possible of both fiction and non-fiction literature on the sex deviant theme; by sponsoring public discussions on pertinent subjects to be conducted by leading members of the legal, psychiatric, religious and other professions; by advocating a mode of behavior and dress acceptable to society.

2 Education of the public at large through acceptance first of the individual, leading to an eventual breakdown of erroneous taboos and prejudices; through public discussion meetings aforementioned; through dissemination of educational literature on the homosexual theme.

3 Participation in research projects by duly authorized and responsible psychologists, sociologists and other such experts directed towards further knowledge of the homosexual.

4 Investigation of the penal code as it pertains to the homosexual, proposal of changes to provide an equitable handling of cases involving this minority group, and promotion of these changes through due process of law in the state legislatures.

Louÿs. It was an obscure name, chosen because most people wouldn't be able to figure out what it meant. Somehow, lesbians were able to find the organization, and by 1959, there were DOB chapters in major cities across the United States.

Soon after forming, the DOB wrote a mission statement and a statement of purpose, which was published on the first page of every issue of the organization's newsletter, *The Ladder*. In many ways, their purpose mirrored the goals of the Mattachine Society; both organizations wanted to help gay and lesbian people overcome their self-hatred, and they wanted to educate the general public that gay and lesbian people were just like everyone else. Until the late 1960s, the Daughters of Bilitis and the Mattachine Society were the only major gay and lesbian organizations in the United States.

THE LADDER ARTICLE, "FIRE HOSES NEXT?"

For decades, San Francisco has been a mecca for gay and lesbian people. Even going back to 1951, San Francisco city ordinances allowed gay people to assemble in public places. That meant that gay bars, clubs, and other social spaces could legally operate in the city. Despite the ordinance, Mayor George Christopher decided to flex his political muscles and wage war on the gay community. He orchestrated a campaign to shut down gay bars and to do whatever he could to drive gay people out of San Francisco. Raids became a regular occurrence, and some of the bars were forced to close their doors.

At about 3:15 a.m. on September 14, 1961, police raided a one-room after-hours club called the Tay-Bush Inn, located on the corner of Taylor and Bush Streets. More than two hundred people were packed inside the bar at the time. According to witnesses, the police let the "respectable-looking people" go, along with those who had political connections. Then they rounded up and arrested the rest. In the end, 103 people (89 men and 14 women) were arrested and taken to jail. As if that wasn't bad enough, the *San Francisco Examiner* ran a story listing every one of their names, addresses, and places of employment. It was the largest vice raid in San Francisco history, and it was intended to scare gay people into hiding.

The mayor's strategy unexpectedly backfired. The *San Francisco Chronicle*, particularly columnist Herb Caen, famously criticized the mayor for picking on gays and lesbians while pardoning gay men who were rich and well connected. If anything, the raid fired them up. The local chapter of the Mattachine Society quickly became active in restoring the gay community's right to assemble.

EDITORIAL

Fire Hoses Next?

There seem to be two different approaches to the conditions at a "gay bar" known as the Tay-Bush Cafe in San Francisco - one, the investigation of safety regulation violations by the Fire Department at the behest of Paul A. Bissinger, police commissioner; the other, a raid on the occupants and the arrest on August 13 of 103 persons on charges of "visiting a disorderly house" (a few being booked additionally for "lewd dancing").

Investigation of safety conditions would certainly appear to be in order regardless of the conflicting claims as to the number of persons on the premises at the time of the raid - Owner Robert Johnson says 242, while the police hold that there could not have been more than 110 in the place, which has four tables and 16 seats at a counter.

But does the investigation for the safety of the patrons require a raid on and the wholesale arrest of said patrons? Are we to believe that the public welfare is served by dragging 89 men and 14 women to jail and booking them on the questionable charge of "visiting a disorderly house"? Is it not possible that the alleged fire hazard could be circumvented by other means than exchanging the crowded conditions of a cafe for the crowded conditions of the city jail? The New York City Fire Department puts a limit on the number of patrons a cafe may "safely" serve. And certainly the cafe owners in that city are forewarned as to existing hazardous conditions. This would seem the more sensible approach to the problem - to safeguard the public by preventing hazard - than to wait until a cafe has extended its patronage beyond its "safe" capacity.

Perhaps there was a side issue in the case which seemed more important to the raiders than "public safety." It is reported that Police Sergeant James Ludlow, in plain-clothes, gave the pre-arranged signal for the raid at the Tay-Bush after observing things from inside for an hour. He said he was influenced by the sight of 25 couples dancing, and only one person was a woman.

So the spark that turned in the "fire alarm" was the sight of men dancing with men - a "fire hazard" indeed. That men were dancing with men is denied by the owner, who says with so many in so small a place it would be an impossibility. That if men were dancing with men and such was more important to the police than the "safety" of those present is a sorry commentary. That men dancing with men constitutes "lewd dancing" any more than men dancing with women is also open to question. That Mayor George Christopher is still smarting from the embarrassment he has suffered by the "gay bar" police bribe cases and the Wolden accusations that "organized homosexuals" have flourished under his regime is very apparent.

His comment after a meeting with Bissinger following the arrests: "We found as always that some arrests are very difficult of prosecution because courts demand total, complete, and unequivocal evidence, but we think we're on the right track."

The "right track," Mr. Mayor, would be to recognize that San Francisco has a very able Fire Department, quite capable of dealing with hazardous conditions which come under its jurisdiction. The "right track" would be to define the duties and draw the line where the jurisdiction of one department ends and the other begins. For too long San Francisco has been subjected to interdepartmental bungling - as in the use of fire hoses by the police department in the so-called "student riots" and in the arrest of 103 persons to circumvent a fire hazard.

The "right track," Mr. Mayor, would be to allow San Francisco's Fire Department to function. They know better than to fight fire with fire. There's water - and sometimes there is negotiation, admission of error and the desire to alleviate undesirable conditions. And sometimes there may even be understanding - and progress!

- Del Martin

14

15

If anything, the Tay-Bush raid brought Mayor Christopher's worst nightmare closer to becoming a reality. That same year, José Sarria, a drag performer at the Black Cat (and also known as the Nightingale of Montgomery Street) decided to run for a seat on the San Francisco Board of Supervisors. As the first openly gay candidate running for public office in the United States, a win for Sarria was highly unlikely. But in the wake of the Tay-Bush raid, Sarria did respectably well on election day, demonstrating the power of the gay vote in San Francisco. In San Francisco, this raid marked the beginning of the end of the raids on gay bars.

The October 1961 issue of *The Ladder* featured an article about the Tay-Bush raid, written by Del Martin. The title ("Fire Hoses Next?") eerily foreshadowed the fire hoses that would eventually be turned on the Stonewall Inn.

PHOTOGRAPH, FRANK KAMENY

Fred Kameny (RIGHT); others unidentified

O n the surface, Frank Kameny lived a very conventional life. Born in 1925 in New York City to Ashkenazi Jewish parents, Frank sailed through high school and graduated when he was sixteen years old. He went to Queens College to study physics, but his studies were temporarily interrupted when he was drafted into the U.S. Army during World War II. After the war, he returned to to Queens College, graduating in 1948 with a physics degree. He then continued his studies at Harvard University, earning both a master's degree and a doctorate in astronomy. After a brief teaching stint at Georgetown University, he was offered a job in 1957 by the U.S. Army Map Service. Everything was perfect—until the U.S. Army discovered that Frank Kameny had an arrest record.

What happened? Frank had been traveling cross-country to complete his doctoral research, and he was groped by another man at a San Francisco bus terminal. Plainclothes officers witnessed the incident, and they arrested Kameny for engaging in homosexual behavior. Once the U.S. Army found out about this, they fired him—and a year later, in 1958, Kameny was banned from any U.S. government employment. He appealed the decision, even petitioning the U.S. Supreme Court, but to no avail.

Frank was shocked and stunned. He'd worked so hard to complete his education, and at thirty-three years old, his career was over. This rattled him to the core—and it radicalized him. He knew he was gay, and he also knew that he shouldn't have to suffer for the rest of his life because of it. Frank decided to devote himself to political activism, and he didn't hold a paid job for the rest of his life.

In 1960, Frank and his friend Jack Nichols cofounded the Washington, D.C., chapter of the Mattachine Society. Up until this point, the Mattachine Society was a very secretive organization. Membership lists were heavily protected, and most people didn't use their real names when they attended meetings. In a departure from this level of secrecy, Frank, Jack, and members of the Daughters of Bilitis began to organize pickets, the first of which was at the White House in April of 1965 in protest of Cuban and U.S. government mistreatment of gay and lesbian people. At these pickets, they wore suits and dresses—which may not seem all that radical, from today's perspective. But what was radical was the fact that gay people had come out of hiding and marched with signs in public places. This was the first time in history that a gay organization had participated in a public affirmation of identity. It was groundbreaking, and it changed the face of gay activism.

"GAY IS GOOD" BUTTON

By the 1960s, many gay and lesbian people had internalized the negative attitudes from the larger culture, believing they were sick, immoral, and depraved. Many stayed in hiding, getting married and starting families in order to provide cover for their homosexuality. Often, they tried to change their sexual orientation by seeing a psychologist or psychiatrist. Some received electroshock therapy. Others underwent behavioral therapy, also receiving electric shocks as punishment for being gay. Still others had brain surgery, including prefrontal lobotomies—many of which caused permanent brain damage. All of these treatments were incredibly barbaric. And none of them worked.

GAY IS GOOD
DRUM

When people are treated badly, it's not uncommon for them to start believing that it's because they're bad. That was happening to the gay community, as well as other marginalized and oppressed groups. For centuries, African Americans, particularly in the United States and in Western

Europe, were led to believe that their skin was too dark, their hair was too coarse and unruly, their noses were too wide, their lips were too big—that everything about them was unattractive and bad. These attitudes date all the way back to slavery. African Americans who had lighter skin, smoother hair, and European facial features were treated better than those who didn't have those features. In fact, some were able to pass as white and escape the clutches of slavery altogether. As a result, throughout the early twentieth century, many African Americans, marinating in the oppressive attitudes of the larger culture, believed that white people were better than black people.

That brings us to the Black Is Beautiful movement. While that phrase (and variations of it) can be traced back to the mid-1800s, the slogan took off in the mid-1960s as the civil rights movement gained traction. Instead of assimilating and trying to "look white," black people tossed aside the skin-bleaching creams and hot combs and began to embrace their natural appearance. Throughout the 1960s and 1970s, the Afro became a powerful symbol of pride, activism, and resistance against oppression.

Frank Kameny and Craig Rodwell saw a similar phenomenon occurring in the gay community. "Most Americans are repelled by the mere notion of homosexuality," reported Mike Wallace in the 1967 CBS documentary *The Homosexuals*. "A CBS poll shows two out of three Americans look on homosexuality with disgust, discomfort, or fear." And that's how many gay and lesbian people viewed themselves—with disgust, discomfort, and fear. As Kameny became more politically active, he realized that picketing wasn't going to be enough; the negative attitudes that homosexuals were internalizing also needed to be challenged. So he coined a new slogan: Gay Is Good.

"Gay Is Good" was the first positive slogan used to describe the gay community. At pickets, Frank Kameny carried signs bearing the phrase. Craig Rodwell, who owned the Oscar Wilde Memorial Bookshop in New York City, used the gay bookstore as a platform to sell the slogan. He posted GAY IS GOOD signs in the window, he ran "Gay Is Good" ads in gay publications, and eventually he sold "Gay Is Good" buttons, stickers, and patches in the store. While the slogan never became as widespread as Black Is Beautiful, it marked a shift in the way that gay and lesbian people presented themselves to the public. Being gay wasn't something to hide, or to be ashamed of. Instead, it was something beautiful and good.

BARBARA GITTINGS'S DRESS, ANNUAL REMINDER

Barbara Gittings (CENTER); others unidentified

fter the April 17, 1965, picket at the White House, Mattachine Society–New York member Craig Rodwell proposed the idea of an annual picket to be held on Independence Day. A number of groups, including the Daughters of Bilitis and the New York City and Washington, D.C., chapters of the Mattachine Society, formed a larger umbrella group called East Coast Homophile Organizations (ECHO), which organized these Annual Reminder events—reminders that gay and lesbian people were denied the rights of life, liberty, and the pursuit of happiness. On July 4, 1965, gay activists, adhering to a strict dress code of dresses for women and jackets and ties for men, carried their signs and marched at Independence Hall in Philadelphia. In this image, Barbara Gittings, one of the members of the Daughters of Bilitis, is wearing a dress, and the men are following the dress code as well.

As radical as this event was, there was almost zero news coverage of the Annual Reminders, and what little coverage existed was negative and sensationalistic. *Confidential* magazine, a tabloid-style publication, ran a story in its October 1965 issue titled "Homos on the March"—a headline that was more likely to grab attention than make readers take gay and lesbian rights seriously. It took courage for gay and lesbian people to publicly advocate for their rights, but the Annual Reminders ultimately didn't have the impact they'd hoped for.

MATCHBOOK, GENE COMPTON'S CAFETERIA

t was a warm night in Los Angeles in May of 1959. Cooper's Donuts was bustling as if it were serving the early morning breakfast crowd. Drag queens sat at the counter sipping coffee, smoking cigarettes, eating a late-night snack, and enjoying each other's company. And then the police came.

Cooper's Donuts was situated between two gay bars—Harold's and the Waldorf—on Main Street in the Skid Row neighborhood of Los Angeles. Skid Row was home to people who lived on the margins of society, such as homeless people, drug addicts, and sexual and gender deviants. Cooper's was a hangout for trans women and drag queens, which also made it a target for the Los Angeles Police Department. On that particular

"The Food You Like"

Gene Compton's
SAN FRANCISCO
333 Geary St.
144 Ellis St. 8-10 Kearny St.
45 Powell St.
Oakland 12th & Broadway
All Stores Open
Day & Night

CLOSE COVER BEFORE STRIKING MATCH

night in May of 1959, two police officers entered the shop and demanded to see the patrons' IDs. This was clearly a harassment tactic—back then, the law in Los Angeles stated that if your gender presentation didn't match the gender on your ID, you could be arrested and taken to jail. And that's exactly what the officers did. When they attempted to arrest five individuals, bystanders began to protest, throwing coffee cups, spoons, and whatever else they had on hand at the police. The police drove off without the people they'd arrested. One of those arrested (but not taken to jail) was a man named John Rechy, a Mexican American novelist who wrote about the raid at Cooper's in his novel *City of Night*.

A few years later, in San Francisco, a similar incident occurred, this time at Gene Compton's Cafeteria. Gene Compton's was located in the Tenderloin area of San Francisco, a seedy red-light district filled with bars and residential hotels. It was one of the few places in the city where drag queens could live openly—and make money in a variety of illegal ways, including prostitution and selling drugs. Compton's, located at 101 Taylor Street, was open twenty-four hours a day, making it a favorite among those who lived in the underbelly of San Francisco. But the management at Compton's didn't want the cafeteria to be a hangout for the queens, so employees routinely called the police to clear the place out. Drag queens were harassed by the police and arrested for a variety of infractions, most often for violating section 240.35, subdivision 4 of the California Penal Code: "Being masked or in any manner disguised by unusual or unnatural attire or facial alteration; loiters, remains, or congregates in a public place with other persons so masked . . ."

In 1966, resistance was in the air. The civil rights movement had been underway for quite some time, and young people were beginning to organize antiwar protests. Leaders at Glide Memorial United Methodist Church, located across the street from Compton's, became a hub of a range of social

---

The civil rights movement started during the Reconstruction era after the Civil War and gained momentum in the 1950s and 1960s. Civil rights activists worked to end racial discrimination and segregation, as well as to secure voting rights for African Americans.

After the United States became involved in the Vietnam War and started bombing North Vietnam, protests against the war began to escalate. The war was expensive, and tens of thousands of U.S. soldiers had either been killed or were wounded. Demonstrations against the war took place throughout the United States.

---

justice efforts. And in July 1966, a group of gay youth and drag queens calling themselves Vanguard protested outside of Compton's for routinely kicking them out and calling the police on them. After that, tensions were high, which brings us to an early morning in August of 1966.

No one knows exactly what date the Compton's Cafeteria Riots took place. The news media didn't cover it when it happened, and police records dating back that far have since been destroyed. However, we do know this: One morning in August of 1966, a Compton's employee called the police to get the drag queens out. When the police arrived, an officer grabbed one of the drag queens, who responded by throwing a cup of coffee in his face. The restaurant erupted in complete pandemonium. Patrons threw plates, salt and pepper shakers, and furniture, smashing the front plate-glass window into smithereens. Drag queens whacked police officers with their purses and high heeled shoes. When the police started making arrests, the fighting spilled out into the street. The drag queens busted the windows of a police car, lit a newsstand on fire, and resisted being loaded into the paddy wagons. It was clear that the drag queens who frequented Compton's were sick and tired of being harassed, and they were ready to fight back. The riots continued on the next night and into the early morning hours. An even larger crowd picketed outside Compton's, and by the end of the protest, the newly installed plate-glass windows had been shattered again. Infuriated, Vanguard members responded by organizing a street sweep—with brooms in hand, they mimicked the police who conducted routine sweeps of city neighborhoods to shoo them away. Unfortunately, their actions weren't enough to spark a social movement.

Even though the riot at Cooper's Donuts and the Compton's Cafeteria Riots predated the Stonewall Riots by several years, both have been a part of LGBT history that has largely been ignored.

BLACK CAT TAVERN RAID LEAFLET

I t was New Year's Eve 1967 at the Black Cat Tavern, a gay bar in Los Angeles. Guests celebrated the approaching new year in their best party attire, wearing gold, silver, and sequins. Moments before the stroke of midnight, the band began to play:

> *Should old acquaintance be forgot,*
> *and never brought to mind?*
> *Should old acquaintance be forgot,*
> *and auld lang syne?*
> *For auld lang syne, my dear,*
> *for auld lang syne.*
> *We'll take a cup of kindness yet,*
> *for auld lang syne.*

The crowd cheered. Partygoers began exchanging the celebratory midnight kiss—a tradition that's said to offer protection from loneliness.

Then, *BAM!!!* The beatings started, and the party ended.

By 1967, police raids of gay bars were happening more frequently. That particular night, the raid was led by undercover LAPD officers posing as bar patrons. Right at the moment when the men in attendance began kissing, the officers blew their cover and pounced. This led to an attack on the gay community that was much more violent than most raids had been before. Two gay men were arrested for kissing, and numerous partygoers were beaten. One of the bartenders was injured so badly he had to go to the hospital. What should have been an evening of celebration turned into a night of terror.

This time, though, the gay community wasn't going down without a fight. A local organization called PRIDE (Personal Rights in Defense and Education) began to organize a series of gay rights protests against police brutality. The first of these protests was held a week after the Black Cat Tavern raid, and others took place throughout January and February of 1967. The flyer shown in this entry was distributed throughout the Los Angeles area, encouraging people to participate in what turned out to be, at least at the time, one of the largest gay rights

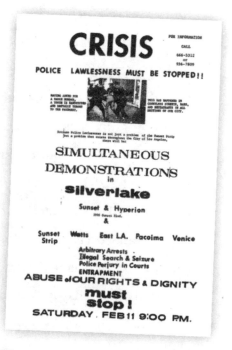

demonstrations in history. Protestors gathered outside of the Black Cat Tavern, chanting and carrying protest signs. Considering how dangerous it was for people at that time to be openly gay, this was a radical move for the gay community. But gay people were getting tired of being hassled by the police, and they knew that staying silent wasn't going to change anything.

Founded in 1966 by Steve Ginsburg, PRIDE was a much more radical group than the Mattachine Society. After the Black Cat raid, Ginsburg and other PRIDE members seized the opportunity to tap into the anger people in the gay community were experiencing. Hoping to increase their numbers, PRIDE members started distributing their newsletters at the 1967 protests, spreading the word about the work they were doing. That's how Richard Mitch (who used the pseudonym Dick Michaels to protect himself) and Bill Rau (otherwise known as Bill Rand) learned of the organization, and they took a special interest in the newsletter. The two men joined PRIDE, took over the newsletter, and in September of 1967 rebranded it as the *Los Angeles Advocate*. Two years later, the newspaper was renamed *The Advocate* and distributed nationally, and today it is one of the most widely read LGBT magazines in the world.

PHOTOGRAPH, SIP-IN AT JULIUS' BAR

F or a long time, people acted as if being gay was a disease you could catch just by seeing it or being around it. But if you couldn't see it, then you couldn't catch it—and that's what shaped many of the laws and policies that forced gay and lesbian people into the closet. In fact, if these laws hadn't existed, then the Stonewall Riots probably would never have happened.

In the 1960s, a gay person couldn't walk into a bar and order a drink. In New York, the State Liquor Authority (SLA) had a regulation on the books that prohibited bars from serving drinks to people who were known or suspected to be gay or lesbian. Even if a person looked gay (whatever that means), bars could refuse to serve that individual. Laws like this had powerful effects. They denied gay and lesbian people any opportunity to meet each other in popular places like cafés, clubs, and bars. To make matters worse, the unspoken assumption was that just being gay was a form of disorderly behavior, a particularly cruel form of oppression that pushed the gay community further into the shadows.

Dick Leitsch and Craig Rodwell, the president and vice president of the Mattachine Society of New York, had

had enough of being pushed around. They decided to take action—but in a bolder way than the "be quiet and behave yourself" approach the Mattachine Society typically used. On April 21, 1966, Dick, Craig, and their friend John Timmons went barhopping in Greenwich Village. But this was no ordinary bar crawl—this was a direct action they called a sip-in. The plan was to go to a number of bars, announce that they were homosexuals, and order a drink. The big question was: Would they be served, or would they be denied service, escorted out of the bar, or arrested? Their hope was that they'd be refused service, because then they could make a formal complaint to the SLA, and ultimately try to change the law. In the hopes that the sip-in would be covered by the media, they contacted four newspaper reporters including journalist Thomas Johnson from the *New York Times* and photographer Fred McDarrah from the *Village Voice*.

The first stop on their itinerary was a place called the Ukrainian American Village Restaurant. This bar had a sign that said IF YOU ARE GAY, PLEASE GO AWAY, which, of course, made them want to go there! Thomas Johnson arrived a few minutes before the others, and without thinking about it, blew the operation by telling the bar owner why he was there. The owner, having no intention of serving gay men at his establishment, closed up shop before Dick, Craig, and John arrived. Strike one.

The three men, along with Thomas Johnson and Fred McDarrah, headed to their second destination, a bar called Dom's. It, too, had a sign telling people to go away if they were gay. And it, too, was closed. Strike two.

The group decided to go for the sure thing. Howard Johnson's, housed in a building with a bright orange roof at the intersection of 8th Street and Sixth Avenue, never closed. After the men were seated, they handed their server a written statement that said: "We are homosexuals. We believe that a place of public accommodation has an obligation to serve an orderly person, and that we are entitled to service so long as we are orderly." The waitress, unsure of what to do, called the manager over, who promptly told her to go ahead and serve them. Victory! Except being served wasn't their goal. They *wanted* to be denied service so they could publicize the injustices that gay people faced.

When they finished their drinks, they headed to a tiki bar called Waikiki's, where the bartender not only served them, but gave them their drinks on the house. The men began to wonder: Would anyone refuse them, or would they end up drunk by the end of the day?

At this point in the bar crawl, their friend Randy Wicker joined them, and the four men headed to Julius' Bar, located about a block away from the Stonewall Inn. There had been a police raid there several days before, and the men knew that it was highly likely that they'd be refused service. The men approached the bar, and the bartender began to set glasses out for them. Then Dick announced that they were gay—and the bartender put his hand over a glass and refused to serve them. That iconic moment was captured by Fred McDarrah, the *Village Voice* photographer.

Thomas Johnson, the reporter from the *New York Times*, provided the news coverage the men were hoping for, but in a not-so-flattering way. The story opened with the headline: "3 Deviates Invite Exclusion by Bars." The *Village Voice* wrote a story about the sip-ins a couple of weeks later. For the first time, discrimination against gay and lesbian people in bars was getting media coverage, and it forced government officials and policymakers to address the issue.

(LEFT TO RIGHT) John Timmons (WITH JACKET ON SHOULDER), Dick Leitsch, Craig Rodwell, Randy Wicker; bartender unidentified

MUG SHOT,
ED "THE SKULL" MURPHY

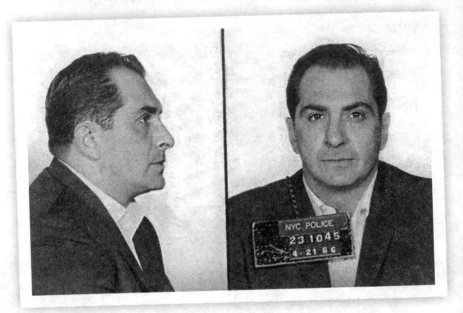

T hroughout the 1960s, the Mafia had almost complete control over the gay social scene in New York City. They figured out early on that they could purchase cheap properties in the city, turn them into gay bars, and get around state liquor laws by operating as private bottle clubs, which were organizations where membership was required. People, particularly those in the Mafia, used this designation as a way to avoid getting a liquor license. Liquor licenses were expensive, and they could also be taken away if there was evidence of openly gay people being served. There was nothing private or clubby about these establishments, though—if anything, they were sleazy and run-down. In order to maintain the pretense of being a club, patrons were required to sign in before entering (and they usually did so with a fake name so their sexual identity wouldn't be discovered by others). This is how the Stonewall Inn operated.

As you know, the Stonewall Inn, prior to becoming a gay bar, was originally livery stables, then it was renovated and turned into a speakeasy, then a legitimate cocktail bar and restaurant. The restaurant, called Bonnie's Stone Wall, was in business until 1966, until a fire all but destroyed the property. That's when Tony Lauria (otherwise known as Fat Tony) purchased the property. (Interestingly, both gay men and mobsters used fake names or nicknames so that they could stay under the radar—gay men from homophobia, mobsters from the law.) Fat Tony did a cheap renovation on the property, and a year later he reopened the Stonewall Inn as a gay bar. The place, in a word, was a dump. The glasses were dirty, there was no running water behind the bar, and there were numerous violations of health, safety, and fire codes.

Even though Fat Tony owned the bar, he was just the front man. Matthew "Matty the Horse" Ianniello, the capo (leader) of the Genovese crime family, was the man behind the operation. Mobsters, particularly the Genovese family, knew they could make money by running gay bars on the underground, and that these bars could serve as fronts for other illegal activities, such as extortion, gambling, and drug dealing. By the 1960s, New York City was littered with dark, seedy gay bars with sticky floors and overpriced drinks, and the Stonewall Inn was one of them. Matty the Horse owned most of the gay bars and clubs in New York City, and he bribed the police with large sums of money so they would leave them alone. He paid the NYPD about two thousand dollars a month to protect the Stonewall Inn. If Matty the Horse paid the police that much for every bar he owned, that adds up to hundreds of thousands of dollars per year. And even with those large payoffs, the police still raided the bars on a regular basis.

How did the Stonewall Inn make a profit if Matty the Horse was giving that much money to the police? For starters, they sold alcohol that was stolen or bootlegged, and the drinks they served were expensive and watered-down. But the real money came from extortion, and Ed "The Skull" Murphy, one of the crew members in the Genovese crime family, was the ringleader. A former pro wrestler, Ed "The Skull" worked elaborate blackmailing schemes, entrapping homosexual male patrons at the Inn. He'd steal patrons' wallets to discover their identity, then send his gangster friends to the unsuspecting patron's home posing as officers from the police morals squad. They would keep quiet, they'd tell him, but for a price. This was how the Stonewall Inn made the big bucks—by shamelessly exploiting their patrons who were doing their best to live in secrecy.

Ed "The Skull" was the bouncer at the door the night of the Stonewall Riots. In 1978, he declared that his criminal career was over, and he came out as a gay man! Afterward, Ed started speaking publicly about gay rights, and he got involved in organizing the annual Christopher Street Festival. After his death in 1989, a block of the AIDS Memorial Quilt, a massive quilt honoring those who died of AIDS, was made in Ed Murphy's name.

DOROTHY'S DRESS, THE WIZARD OF OZ

n the 1950s and 1960s, Judy Garland, the actress who played Dorothy in the classic film *The Wizard of Oz*, was the darling of the gay community. Judy died on June 22, 1969, and her funeral, coincidentally, was held the day the Stonewall Riots erupted. Some believe that the gay community, riddled with grief, was more than ready for an uprising—and that's exactly what happened that night. "You could actually feel it in the air. You really could," Sylvia Rivera said, describing the atmosphere after Judy Garland's death, in a 2009 interview. Although many historians challenge the idea that Judy Garland's funeral was what actually sparked the riots, there's no question about Judy's status as the quintessential icon of the gay community at the time. Back in the 1950s and 1960s, it was customary to use the phrase "friend of Dorothy" to refer to a gay person. In fact, when people signed in at the Stonewall, Judy Garland was one of the most common pseudonyms used.

Why Judy Garland, and why *The Wizard of Oz*? In the movie, before the tornado hits, Dorothy dreams of a life outside of Kansas, in a place that's accepting and more exciting, colorful, and filled with adventure—and in that scene, she sings "Over the Rainbow," a song whose message resonates strongly with LGBT people. It's obviously no accident that the rainbow flag has become a worldwide symbol for the LGBT community—it clearly reflects the promise of a land "somewhere over the rainbow," where they would be welcomed, no matter what.

When Dorothy arrives in the Land of Oz, she meets Glinda the Good Witch (who kind of looks like a drag queen) and the Munchkins (who come out when Glinda calls them). As she travels down the Yellow Brick Road, Dorothy meets the Scarecrow, the Tin Man, and the Cowardly Lion, a ragtag group of misfits who don't fit in anywhere, and who are all looking for that one thing that will make them happy. And despite their eccentricities, Dorothy accepts all of them unconditionally.

Is Glinda the Good Witch a drag queen? Are the Munchkins "coming out" of the closet? Is the Cowardly Lion secretly gay, and searching for the courage to be himself? Perhaps all of this is spot-on. Or perhaps we're reading into the film way too much. Whatever the case, many people in the LGBT community see themselves and their experiences reflected in *The Wizard of Oz*, and Judy Garland has come to embody that sense of validation.

Today, a replica of Dorothy's blue-and-white-checkered dress hangs in the window of the Stonewall Inn. It serves as a reminder of Judy Garland's death prior to the Stonewall Riots, and of what Judy has symbolized for the gay community.

THE
RIOTS

By the 1960s, the seeds of the gay liberation movement had been planted. But gay rights was by no means the only focus during that time period. The civil rights movement had been underway for well over a decade, and by the mid-1960s, Black Power became the focus. Alongside the Black Power movement, people (primarily students) were protesting the Vietnam War and advocating for free speech. Mexican Americans were leading El Movimiento, fighting for farmworker rights, education, and the dismantling of ethnic stereotypes. The women's movement kicked into high gear in the 1960s. Everything was being questioned, giving rise to a vibrant counterculture expressed through clothing, art, hairstyles, and music. People began to mistrust the media, and underground newspapers and alternative presses began to crop up. Instead of engaging in traditional forms of political activity, people favored direct actions like protests, sit-ins, teach-ins, rallies, demonstrations, pickets, petitions, marches, and boycotts. In Greenwich Village, the raid and subsequent protest at the Stonewall Inn was a flashpoint that launched a more radical gay rights movement.

What actually happened on June 28, 1969? We know that the police raided the Stonewall Inn. We know that people fought back, instead of yielding to the police. We have some photographic evidence of the aftermath of the raid, some of which was taken by *Village Voice* photographer Fred McDarrah, others of which were captured by a freelance photographer named Diana Davies. We also have a few news articles about the rebellion, one of which was a first-person account by Howard Smith. That's about all the evidence we have.

Unfortunately, many people who were there that night have died, so we can't ask them. And there's intense disagreement among the people who were there (or who claim to have been there) about what actually occurred. If an event like this had taken place today, bystanders would have used their cell phones to film each moment.

What do people disagree about? Some say that Marsha P. Johnson, an African American drag queen and activist, was at the Stonewall Inn celebrating her birthday that night, and that she threw the first brick. Others point out that Marsha's birthday was on August 24, not June 28—and that not only did she not throw the first brick, no one threw bricks, because there were no bricks lying around waiting to be thrown. Estimates of how many people participated in the rebellion range from a couple hundred to several thousand. Some insist that the gay community's grief over Judy Garland's death caused bar patrons to fight back, while others feel that chalking the riots up to Judy Garland cheapens the anger and frustration gay people had about being harassed and persecuted. And then there's the ever-present argument about whether the rebellion was started by lesbians, transvestites, street kids, and people of color, or whether the upheaval was part of the gay rights movement led predominantly by white gay men. Those disagreements, really, are just the tip of the iceberg. The reality is that no one remembers exactly what happened that night. And because most newspapers didn't cover the events, and most journalists didn't interview people who participated, we have very few documented accounts of the Stonewall raid and rebellion.

Why are there so many conflicting reports about what happened? Some of it may have to do with the fleeting, unstable nature of human memory. If you've ever gotten into an argument with someone because you remembered an event one way and the other person remembered it completely differently, you understand the problem. People tend to trust the accuracy of their memories more than they trust the accuracy of facts, especially when the memory is of an emotionally charged event. They remember the event itself, and they remember it vividly. There's no doubt, obviously, that the Stonewall Inn was raided by the police, and that bar patrons and people on the street fought back and resisted. However, memory for emotional events is like tunnel vision; the brain holds on to the main event, but at the expense of the details. And that may well be why people continue to argue about the details of the Stonewall rebellion. However, what is abundantly clear is that the Stonewall rebellion marked a turning point in LGBT history.

NYPD OFFICIAL POLICE HAT, CIRCA 1960S

Gay bars, particularly those run by the mob, were regularly raided by the police. Not only were these raids an opportunity to bust the Mafia, they were a way for officers to pad their arrest numbers. High arrest numbers were desirable because they reassured the public that their city was becoming safer now that criminals were off the streets. According to Deputy Inspector Seymour Pine, who led the raid on the Stonewall Inn, gay people "were easy arrests. They never gave you any trouble." Although that certainly wasn't true early in the morning on June 28, 1969.

Seymour Pine was a deputy inspector for the vice and gambling unit (the morals squad) of the NYPD's Sixth Precinct, which was located in Greenwich Village. The Sixth Precinct received regular payoffs from the owners of the Stonewall Inn, but raids happened anyway. Early in the morning on June 28, 1969, the officers at the Sixth Precinct had received a tip about a Mafia racket involving stolen European bonds, and that bars and clubs like the Stonewall Inn were mixed up in the operation. The Stonewall was a front for a wide range of illegal activities, including money laundering (making money that came from an illegal source look like it came from someplace legal), gambling, drug dealing, and processing stolen goods. The police knew this, and for that reason, police officers dressed in plainclothes were always inside the Stonewall, looking for signs of illegal activity.

The night started off like any other. There were four officers inside the bar; two plainclothes policewomen posing as lesbians, and two plainclothes male officers as gay men. Pine and his partner, Detective Charles Smythe, were across the street from the bar in Christopher Street Park. Typically, one of the officers inside would give a signal indicating that it was time to raid the bar. This time, according to Pine, that signal never came. "It got to the point that either they were in trouble or they had forgotten what they were supposed to do," Pine said.

Pine and Smythe decided to go in. They figured that they could rationalize a bar raid because there were people under the age of twenty-one inside. When they entered the bar, Pine and Smythe thought that the patrons would obediently line up and march out—just like usual. Very quickly, they discovered that there was nothing typical about this particular raid.

Word got out that the bar was being raided, and a crowd of people began to gather outside. Before they knew it, the officers were trapped inside, and the scene erupted into pandemonium.

Here's Pine's account of the event: "It was very scary. I had a group [of officers] completely scared. The cobblestones that [*sic*] were being thrown and the bottles being thrown when we moved back inside. We knew we were in trouble. I was concerned that someone wouldn't [*sic*] lose their cool. If someone pulled a trigger, we were dead—because they would've just run over us. They were throwing Molotov cocktails in there, but we put that [*sic*] out."

Finally, one of the female officers escaped through a vent in the rear of the building and radioed the Sixth Precinct for help. According to Pine, the officers from the Sixth Precinct took their sweet time to show up—probably taking revenge because Pine didn't tell them he was going to raid the bar. Eventually, two police wagons showed up, and Pine felt it was safe enough for those trapped inside to exit the building.

Seymour Pine retired from the Sixth Precinct in 1976. He died in 2010 at the age of ninety-one. Before he died, Pine apologized to the gay community for leading the raid. But he also was quoted as saying, "If what I did helped gay people, then I'm glad."

NYPD-ISSUED NIGHTSTICK, CIRCA 1960S

T he officers who were trapped inside the Stonewall Inn were just regular cops. When the officers finally escaped, an elite squad of the NYPD called the Tactical Patrol Force (TPF) arrived and took over the operation. The TPF was formed in 1959 as an experimental squad, mostly to contain street crimes like muggings and robberies. The NYPD viewed the TPF as part of the city's larger strategic plan to suffocate crime, street disturbances, and general unrest. By the 1960s, the TPF was routinely called in to handle things like antiwar protests, civil rights demonstrations, and political sit-ins. They also conducted sweeps—large-scale efforts to rid areas of undesirables—in places like Washington Square Park in Greenwich Village.

In order to qualify for the TPF, officers had to meet very specific standards. They had to be young and tough: The average age of TPF officers was twenty-four, and most of them were at least six feet tall. Military experience was a plus; in many ways, the TPF was more like a military operation than an ordinary police squad. And overwhelmingly, TPF officers were white—which didn't endear them to politically active communities of color in the 1960s.

Once the TPF arrived at the Stonewall Inn, the mood intensified, and the police tactics quickly became violent. TPF officers were dressed in full riot gear, complete with helmets, body shields, and nightsticks. They began swinging their nightsticks at people, often hitting them on the head. This was called "braining"—using a nightstick to strike a person's head with full force. The goal was either to temporarily stun the victim or to knock them unconscious. As you might imagine, this is dangerous and violent, and the practice sometimes caused concussions, skull fractures, and even death.

The nightsticks officers used back in the 1960s were called straight sticks. During the day, officers carried shorter batons; at night, standard-issue NYPD nightsticks were twenty-six inches long and made of solid wood. During the civil rights movement, TPF officers used these nightsticks regularly to subdue crowds, intimidate protestors, and in some cases to cause bodily harm. As various political movements intensified, charges of police brutality began to escalate, and beginning in the 1970s, most police forces began to phase out the straight stick. Today, straight wooden batons are no longer standard issue, and police are prohibited from striking the head, the rib cage, the spine, or the groin unless it's in order to protect someone's life. Instead, officers typically use expandable aluminum batons, which are lighter and much less likely to kill someone or cause serious bodily injury.

PHOTOGRAPH, STORMÉ DELAVERIE

The moment a lesbian woman fought back against the police, the routine police raid turned into an all-out rebellion. But who was that woman? Witnesses who were present on the morning of June 28 say that the police arrested a woman described as "a typical New York butch," and "a dyke-stone butch." (Dyke is a word, typically used as an insult, to describe a lesbian. A butch is a lesbian whose appearance, clothing, behaviors, and mannerisms are more masculine.) After the police arrested this woman, they hand-cuffed her and dragged her from the front of the Stonewall Inn to the paddy wagon—and then she escaped. The police captured her again, dragged her back to the paddy wagon—and she escaped again! This happened a few more times over the course of about ten minutes. Finally, when she screamed that her handcuffs were too tight, an officer hit her over the head with a nightstick. Even though her head was bleeding, the woman continued to fight. Finally, she looked squarely at the crowd and yelled, "Why don't you guys do something?" An officer shoved her into the back of the paddy wagon, which caused the crowd to explode.

Who was this woman?

Some believe that the Stonewall Lesbian might have been Stormé DeLarverie, a well-known drag performer and all-around tough butch. Born in racially segregated New Orleans in 1920, Stormé's father was a wealthy white man, and her African American mother was one of his servants. The kids in school teased Stormé relentlessly for being mixed race, and she learned to protect herself by fighting back. When she was a teenager, Stormé left school and joined the Ringling Bros. circus, jumping horses while riding side-saddle. You have to be tough in order to do that! Unfortunately, even tough people can fall off horses and break bones, and that's what ended Stormé's circus career. After that, during the 1950s and 1960s, Stormé joined a mixed-race drag troupe called the Jewel Box Revue. As the only woman in the troupe (the troupe billed itself as "25 men and 1 girl"), Stormé dressed as a man, while the others dressed as women. The troupe toured the United States and performed regularly at venues like the Apollo Theater and Radio City Music Hall. Stormé became known for her deep voice, her jazz-inspired rhythm, and her gentlemanly persona, all of which made her a recognizable figure in the drag performance circuit.

Stormé was in New York City the night the Stonewall Inn was raided. But was Stormé really the Stonewall Lesbian?

She says she was. So do others, including *New York Times* journalist Charles Kaiser. But others question whether Stormé was in fact that person. For starters, it took thirty years for someone to come forward and identify Stormé as the Stonewall Lesbian. Stormé herself didn't share that information until 2008—thirty-nine years after Stonewall. When asked why she'd stayed silent for all these years, she replied, "Because I didn't think it was anybody's business." A number of witnesses say that the woman who fought with the police was white, not African American or mixed race. In fact, at least one witness says that Stormé wasn't even there that first night—and if she had been, she would have been instantly recognizable.

In June 2009, forty years after the Stonewall Inn was raided, several police reports that were taken that night were released. One report names three people who were arrested: Raymond Castro, Marilyn Fowler, and Vincent DePaul.

Raymond Castro, the first person named in the arrest report, shared his recollections of that night. Amid the commotion, Ray started pushing back against the police, who responded by knocking him down with a nightstick. The police handcuffed him and tried to shove him into the police wagon, but Ray fought back. "I sprung up like a jumping jack and pushed backwards, knocking the police down to the ground, almost against the wall of the Stonewall," Ray said in an interview. Eventually, they dragged him into the wagon and took him to the Sixth Precinct, where he was booked for shoving and kicking a police officer.

The two others named in the report—Marilyn Fowler and Vincent DePaul—have never come forward and are still unidentified. "Vincent DePaul" may not have been that individual's real name. Gay people commonly gave fake names to the police, often names that had some kind of hidden significance. Vincent DePaul was a Catholic saint—ironic, given that most people in the 1960s didn't think of gay people as saintly. Chances are good that whoever Vincent DePaul was, he used his arrest as an opportunity to mess with the police.

That leaves Marilyn Fowler—the woman who was probably the Stonewall Lesbian. Ray Castro described this woman as slim, about five feet, four inches tall, with short black hair, and "not really feminine or masculine." Others who witnessed the events of June 28, 1969, have given similar physical descriptions. But no one has come forward to confirm or establish her identity.

So that's all we have—a police report containing the

name Marilyn Fowler (which could be real or a pseudonym), a couple of eyewitness reports, and a handful of decades-old memories. If anything, we're left with more questions than answers. That's how history works sometimes—it's impossible to nail down all of the details of events that have occurred so many years ago.

PHOTOGRAPH, CRAIG RODWELL INSIDE THE ORIGINAL OSCAR WILDE MEMORIAL BOOKSHOP

I n an interview with WNYC, *Village Voice* reporter Howard Smith described the scene at the bar: "All of a sudden a stone hit the bldg [*sic*]. People started yelling in the crowd a lot. Yelling 'Gay Power!'" The person who led the chant was Craig Rodwell, a gay activist and owner of the Oscar Wilde Memorial Bookshop—the first gay bookstore in the United States.

Rodwell, who was born in 1940 in Chicago, Illinois, had a rough childhood. When he was six years old, he was sent to a Christian Science boarding school. The atmosphere there was bleak, and some of the other kids called Rodwell a "sissy." On a more positive note, Craig learned a lot about the teachings of Christian Science, and he was particularly influenced by the idea that truth is the highest good. Despite the bullying, being at boarding school and away from family judgment allowed Craig to embrace his openly gay identity. In 1958, when Craig was eighteen, he moved to New York City and began volunteering for the Mattachine Society, which he'd heard about while he was in school. His path to activism had begun.

From the beginning, Craig was a radical within the generally cautious homophile movement. In 1961, he began his first serious relationship with a young Harvey Milk, who later moved to San Francisco, was elected to political office, and was ultimately assassinated in 1978. At the time of their relationship, Harvey didn't publicly identify as gay, and he was uncomfortable with Rodwell's revolutionary views, particularly the idea of linking homosexuality to political activism. Shortly after Harvey broke up with him, Craig became depressed and attempted suicide. After being hospitalized for several weeks, he returned home and stepped up his political activity.

Rodwell quickly became a leader in the gay rights movement, and his brand of politics was radically different from the button-up-and-look-good approach of the rest of the Mattachine Society. During a time when most gay activists used pseudonyms to protect themselves from arrest and public humiliation, Rodwell always used his real name. He participated in various pickets, including the 1965 Mattachine Society picket at the White House. The Annual Reminder pickets at Independence Hall in Philadelphia were Craig's idea, and he was one of the principal organizers of that action. He participated with fellow Mattachine Society members in the sip-in at Julius' Bar, even though he'd been thrown out of Julius' a few weeks earlier for wearing an EQUALITY FOR HOMOSEXUALS button. He was a strong advocate for gay youth, leading the Mattachine Young Adults in 1964, and later starting a group called HYMN (Homophile Youth Movement in Neighborhoods).

One of Craig's biggest contributions to the gay rights movement was opening the Oscar Wilde Memorial Bookshop in November 1967. Originally located at 291 Mercer Street, across from Washington Square Park, the bookstore was a place where people could find materials written by gay and lesbian authors and get accurate information about homosexuality. Craig didn't want homosexuality to be hidden in the shadows anymore, and he didn't want gay and lesbian people to feel ashamed about their identities. The Oscar Wilde Memorial Bookshop served as a gathering space for activists, a fundraising hub, an informal counseling center, and a place where gay and lesbian people could find each other.

In 1973, Craig moved the Oscar Wilde Memorial Bookshop out of the tiny storefront at 291 Mercer Street to a larger space on the corner of Christopher Street and Gay Street. He sold the bookstore in 1993, three months before he died of stomach cancer. The Oscar Wilde Memorial Bookshop remained open until 2009, when it closed its doors permanently.

ARREST RECORD, DAVE VAN RONK

I n the late 1960s, Greenwich Village was a nerve center of creativity, counterculture, and direct political action. Musicians, artists, political activists, hippies, war protestors, feminists, Black Panther Party members, and gay activists commingled in the streets of the Village. This is the backdrop for how Dave Van Ronk comes into the story.

Dave Van Ronk was a folk singer and Greenwich Village resident who embodied many elements of this rising counterculture. His political convictions inspired his music, and he was no stranger to protests. One example: On March 27, 1961, the New York City Parks Commission enacted a ban on performing folk music in Washington Square Park because of the unsavory appearance of the musicians. People were outraged, and in response, on April 9, 1961, hundreds of folk musicians gathered in Washington Square Park, guitars in hand, to protest the ban. The paddy wagons and mounted police arrived on the scene, and what started off as a peaceful protest turned into the Beatnik Riot. Several people were arrested, and dozens were roughed up by the police. But the musicians didn't give up— for weeks, they continued to play in Washington Square

Park, and finally, the city relented and repealed the ban on folk music. Clearly, folk music represented a challenge to the mainstream music scene; in fact, Van Ronk himself referred to the early 1960s as the Great Folk Scare, after the Red Scare.

In 1969, Van Ronk lived at 190 Waverly Place, next door to Julius' Bar, and a block away from the Stonewall Inn. His apartment was a gathering space for established and up-and-coming folk singers, and he was a mentor to many rising stars, including Bob Dylan. The night the Stonewall Inn was raided, Van Ronk was at a nearby bar called the Lion's Head Tavern, a popular hangout for writers, artists, folk singers, and political activists. When he left the bar, Van Ronk witnessed the activity outside the Stonewall Inn. "I was passing by and I saw what was going down," he said in an interview, "and I figured, they can't have a riot without me!" Van Ronk wasn't gay, but he had firsthand experience with police violence, both at the Beatnik Riot and at various antiwar demonstrations. "As far as I was concerned," said Van Ronk, "anybody who'd stand against the cops was all right with me, and that's why I stayed in . . . Every time you turned around the cops were pulling some outrage or another."

The crowds swelled to about five hundred people, and the police were clearly outnumbered. To escape the frenzy, officers grabbed some of the protestors (including Van Ronk), dragged them into the Stonewall Inn, and barricaded themselves inside, presumably for their safety. This is how Howard Smith, the reporter who was trapped inside the Stonewall Inn with the police, described the scene:

Pine, a man of about 40 and smallish build, gathers himself, leaps out into the melee, and grabs someone around the waist, pulling him downward and back into the doorway. They fall. Pine regains hold and drags the elected protester inside by the hair. The door slams again. Angry cops converge on the guy, releasing their anger on this sample from the mob. Pine is saying, "I saw him throwing something," and the guy unfortunately is giving some sass, snidely admits to throwing "only a few coins." The cop who was cut is incensed, yells something like, "So you're the one who hit me!" And while the other cops help, he slaps the prisoner five or six times very hard and finishes with a punch to the mouth. They handcuff the guy as he almost passes out. "All right," Pine announces, "we book him for assault."

The person who was booked for assault—and who was dragged inside by his hair, slapped around several times, and punched in the mouth by the police—was Dave Van Ronk. The police report (which incorrectly identified the folk singer as an actor) indicates that Van Ronk was arrested for hitting an officer in the face "with an unknown object." Van Ronk eventually pleaded guilty to harassment, and he was later sued by the officer he allegedly assaulted.

Van Ronk continued to record music until his death on February 10, 2002. In 2004, a section of Sheridan Square, where Barrow Street meets Washington Place, was renamed Dave Van Ronk Street in his memory.

PHOTOGRAPH, 1968 VOLKSWAGEN BEETLE

So many movements were happening at once in the 1960s. There was Black Power, women's liberation, the anti–Vietnam War movement, the free speech movement—and, of course, the gay liberation movement, which gained serious momentum after Stonewall. And there were hippies. Lots of hippies.

Hippies were the heart and soul of the 1960s youth counterculture movement. They were on a quest to become free from the establishment, challenge tradition and authority, and find spiritual meaning in life. Hippies embraced a nomadic lifestyle, establishing communal living spaces throughout the United States. In defiance of capitalistic greed, many hippies made their own clothing, grew and cooked organic and natural food, and rid themselves of material possessions. This antiestablishment, counter-cultural hippie style was characterized by psychedelic art, brightly colored clothing, bell-bottom pants, tie-dyed shirts and dresses, vests, dashikis, peasant blouses, long flowing skirts, head scarves and flower crowns, and beaded jewelry with peace sign medallions. And every self-respecting hippie either owned a Volkswagen Beetle or Bus, or knew someone who did.

While the Volkswagen was very popular in Germany during the 1930s and 1940s, the car didn't sell well in the United States. For starters, the brand was associated with the Nazis. (It was Adolf Hitler who came up with the idea of a car that was simple, mass-produced, and affordable.) On top of that, the Volkswagen Beetle was weird looking, small, and slow. In order to get people to buy Volkswagens, the company distanced itself from its Nazi roots and rebranded the Beetle as

a counterculture car. And it worked. Advertisements for the Beetle portrayed the car as quirky, amusing, and unconventional—the complete opposite of the older generation's dowdy Buick and Pontiac sedans. By the late 1960s, the Beetle had completely divorced itself from its Third Reich origins, and was firmly established as a hippie car.

Let's bring this back to Stonewall. In 1969, there were plenty of Volkswagen Beetles dotting the streets of Greenwich Village. One of them was parked across the street from the Stonewall Inn the morning of June 28, 1969. Later that morning, at about ten o'clock, the owner of the car showed up at the NYPD's Sixth Precinct station house to file a police report. According to the report, their VW Beetle had been "stomped on," damaging the roof, hood, and rear engine cover of the car. The name of the person who made the complaint was blacked out on the report, so their identity is unknown.

We know that there was significant destruction of property as a result of the raid and ensuing riot. However, this is the *only* official report documenting any property damage that night.

PHOTOGRAPH, MARSHA P. JOHNSON

Happy birthday, Marsha! Or was it? Many have claimed that Marsha P. Johnson, who alternated between identifying as gay, a drag queen, and a transvestite, celebrated her birthday at the Stonewall Inn the night of June 28, 1969, and that she threw the first brick.

Marsha's birthday, for the record, wasn't in June. She was born on August 24, 1945, in Elizabeth, New Jersey, and was one of seven children. Her father, Malcolm Michaels Sr., worked at the General Motors factory, and her mother, Alberta Claiborne, cleaned houses for a living. Every week, her family attended services at a local African Methodist Episcopal Church, and they were faithful practicing Christians. On the surface, Marsha, her siblings, and her parents looked like a typical African American family in the 1940s and 1950s. Until Marsha began wearing dresses.

The boys in the neighborhood bullied her relentlessly— enough to make Marsha stop wearing girls' clothing for a time. Her mother once said to Marsha that being homosexual was "lower than a dog." As offensive as that statement is, it was what people believed. Most people at that time considered homosexuality—or any form of gender-bending—to be sick and repulsive. Marsha made it through high school, graduating in 1963, and promptly left for New York City with $15 and a bag of clothes.

Marsha's birth name, Malcolm Michaels Jr., evaporated once she arrived in the city. At first, she called herself "Black Marsha," then later changed it to "Marsha P. Johnson," naming herself after the Howard Johnson's restaurant in Times Square. Howard Johnson's was a national chain of restaurants and hotels known for its bright orange rooftops. As for her middle initial, if anyone asked her what the "P" stood for, Marsha's response was always "Pay it no mind!" In many ways, her name reflects her personality—colorful, spirited, creative, and playful.

Marsha was perpetually homeless, sometimes sleeping on the streets, sometimes staying at gay activist Randy Wicker's apartment. She didn't have a job, so she didn't have any money, and because being a drag queen could get expensive, Marsha had to get creative. Most of her drag outfits came from thrift stores, and she was a pro at finding the most whimsical, colorful items to wear. Sometimes she slept under the tables at the Flower Market on 28th Street between Sixth and Seventh Avenues, and she'd collect discarded flowers and make crowns and garlands out of them.

That brings us to June 28, 1969. Some say that Marsha was inside the Stonewall Inn, celebrating her birthday. (Remember that her birthday was on August 24.) Some say she threw a shot glass at the police, referring to it as "the shot glass that was heard around the world." Others say she threw a brick. Still others say she jumped on top of a car. And some say she wasn't there at all. Johnson herself said that she didn't arrive that first night until about two a.m., after the police had raided the bar. Amid the swirling urban legends, Marsha's account is probably the most accurate.

Whatever her participation was beyond that, two things are possible. Her role in the uprising may have been overembellished or misremembered. It's also possible that her participation in the Stonewall rebellion was downplayed by people in the gay community because of her volatile personality and unstable behavior. Marsha was a complex person, and she wasn't always warm and playful. She suffered from mental illness, and sometimes she could be angry, violent, and short-tempered. People who knew Marsha often referred to her angry persona as Malcolm. She'd been arrested a number of times, and throughout her life she suffered from psychotic breaks that required her to be hospitalized and medicated. Because of her unpredictable behavior, Marsha was banned from entering a number of gay bars in the city.

Marsha was a fierce advocate for gay and trans street kids throughout her life. She was a member of a drag performance troupe called Hot Peaches, and she was famously photographed by Andy Warhol for his *Ladies and Gentlemen* series. Later, Marsha became an AIDS activist and participated in direct actions with ACT UP New York, an advocacy group that worked to end the AIDS crisis and improve the lives of people with AIDS.

NEW YORK CITY PARKING METER, CIRCA 1960S

The night of the raid, instead of complying with the police, the patrons of the bar engaged in various acts of resistance. When the police barricaded themselves inside the Stonewall Inn, activists yanked a parking meter out of the sidewalk and began using it as a battering ram!

Wait . . . let's back up. They *yanked* a parking meter out of the sidewalk—and used it as a battering ram? Parking meters are heavy; a single-space meter like this one weighed anywhere between thirty and fifty pounds, depending on how many coins were inside. Additionally, parking meters were welded to a length of galvanized pipe, which was set in concrete along the sidewalk. Participants at the Stonewall Riots say that a group of people rocked the parking meter back and forth in order to dislodge it, then a beefy muscular guy came along and wrenched it out of the ground. If you think about it,

the collective anger of the crowd was channeled into a serious act of brute strength! Some witnesses remember that there was street construction happening near the Christopher Street subway station, and that the broken concrete in that area may have been where the famous parking meter was uprooted.

PHOTOGRAPH, ROCKETTES, THANKSGIVING DAY PARADE, 1966

The Rockettes have performed at Radio City Music Hall in New York City since the 1930s. A long-standing New York tradition, the Rockettes are best known for their famous kick lines, in perfect eye-high formation. So what does this have to do with Stonewall?

As the first night of the rebellion wore on, the NYPD lined up in a V (also called a wedge formation) and began to descend upon the protestors on Christopher Street. Usually, this would cause rioters to retreat. But this time, they didn't. Instead, they scattered like mice, avoiding the swinging nightsticks, then running behind the wedge formation and throwing bottles, coins, and other objects at the police. When the police reversed formation, they found themselves facing a kick line of cross-dressers, mimicking the Rockettes from Radio City Music Hall. In loud mocking voices, to the tune of the old vaudeville song "Ta-ra-ra Boom-de-ay" (the tune used for the then popular *Howdy Doody Show* theme song), they began to sing:

We are the Stonewall girls
We wear our hair in curls
We wear our dungarees
Above our nelly knees!

There were other versions of the song, some much racier than this. (*Nelly* means feminine.)

Why would the protestors put themselves on the line? For starters, it stopped the riot police in their tracks. This clearly wasn't the kind of reaction the police typically faced, and for a moment, the dumbfounded officers didn't know what to do. It gave the protestors the upper hand, at least for a few minutes. The kick line, complete with flamboyant costumes and off-key singing, also added a dose of humor to the situation. Throughout history, activists have used many tactics to resist oppression, and humor is one of them. Humor is creative, nonviolent, and often unexpected. It's a form of political mischief-making. It exposes the ridiculousness of a situation (because if you think about it, calling in the riot police to beat up a bunch of men dressed as women is pretty ridiculous). For the protestors themselves, humor can be a coping mechanism and a stress reliever. It's a way of creating some breathing room in a high-pressure situation. And it allowed the protestors to mock and torment the police, instead of being the ones who were mocked and tormented.

While the protestors sang and danced, the police slowly advanced forward in formation. But the protestors didn't budge; they stood firm and continued their performance. When the police came within eight feet of them, the kick line broke, and protestors ran in all directions, taking advantage of Greenwich Village's maze of streets. These bob-and-weave tactics made it very difficult for the police to chase the protestors or to contain the crowd. As a result, most were able to escape or resist arrest.

PHOTOGRAPH, MAGOO, BOB KOHLER'S DOG

B ob Kohler was a lifelong New Yorker and activist, living most of his years in an apartment on Charles Street in Greenwich Village. Magoo, a miniature schnauzer, was Bob's best friend. They went on daily walks that took them through Christopher Street Park, and Magoo managed to win the hearts of many of the homeless street kids who hung

out there. Most of these kids were either runaways or had been kicked out of their homes for being gay. Many of them resorted to drug dealing and prostitution to make money. Bob got to know quite a few of those kids during those walks, and he would often give them money, food, or clothing. Being gay himself, Bob could empathize with the rejection and loneliness these kids were experiencing. He was like a father figure, and he never took advantage of them.

In the early morning hours of June 28, 1969, Bob and Magoo were taking a walk down the streets of Greenwich Village. When they approached Christopher Street Park, they were surprised to see a crowd of several hundred people, as well as the police. They were chanting, throwing things, mocking the police officers—and, to Bob's disbelief, being thrown into the police wagon. Things quickly got out of control, and Bob found himself trying to keep Magoo under control amid the chaos. Bob was no stranger to political activity. Beginning in the early 1960s, he was a member of a civil rights group called Congress of Racial Equality (CORE). Later, he became a founding member of the Gay Liberation Front and worked to develop connections and find common ground with the Black Panther Party. Over his lifetime, he participated in the anti-Vietnam War movement, as well as activism for animal rights and environmental causes. On the day of the Christopher Street Liberation Day march, a year after the Stonewall Riots, Magoo walked alongside Bob on the route. Many marchers brought their dogs that day; if police stopped them, they could use their dogs as an excuse: "I'm just taking my dog out for a walk."

Although Bob had several dogs over his lifetime, Magoo had been his favorite. After Magoo died, Bob kept a small figurine of a schnauzer on his fireplace mantle in commemoration of his beloved dog. Bob Kohler himself died on December 5, 2007, and a political funeral was held for him that following Sunday. Participants marched from the Lesbian, Gay, Bisexual, and Transgender Community Center on West 13th Street to the Christopher Street Pier, where they spread his ashes in the Hudson River.

VIEW FROM THE THIRD-FLOOR FIRE ESCAPE AT 84 GROVE STREET

Actress Margot Avery, who was ten years old when the Stonewall Riots occurred, still lives in an apartment at 84 Grove Street, right across the street from Christopher Street Park and the Stonewall Inn. Her babysitter was a student at NYU, and Margot lived on the third floor of the building. The night the Stonewall Inn was raided, Margot, her babysitter, and some of her babysitter's friends watched from the third-floor fire escape of the building, which was like front-row seating. This is how she describes what she saw:

There weren't a lot of people that first night. The Stonewall Inn was tiny. It probably could hold about a hundred people, at most. Christopher Street Park isn't very big, and I remember that there was enough room for people to move around and fight.

I saw a large group of people flamboyantly dressed. I thought they were women, but my babysitter told me they were men. I grew up in the theater, so I knew a lot of gay men and lesbians, but I didn't really understand it. I got that Uncle Ben and Uncle Louie lived together, but I didn't understand that they had a relationship, like my parents. I also didn't know the word "drag queen." I just knew that there were a lot of people out there wearing colorful and extravagant outfits. It was the 1960s, and lots of people dressed outrageously. Back then, the way you dressed was a form of protest in and of itself.

There were more people after that first night. It seemed like a mass of humanity out there. One of the things I remember most vividly was the kick line, which happened

*either the second or third night. Some people question
whether or not the kick line happened, but that's one of the
things I remember most vividly. The people in the kick line
wore brightly colored costumes made with lots of chiffon.
I remember thinking at the time that they looked like a
huge bunch of butterflies. They were singing and dancing,
like the Rockettes at Radio City Music Hall—except they
weren't as choreographed as the Rockettes!*

*The riot police were lined up in formation at the
intersection of Waverly and Christopher Street—the
pointy end of Christopher Street Park. There was only
about ten or twelve feet of space between the cops and the
kick line. I knew about riots and protests, although I'd
never seen one in my neighborhood. Seeing the riot police
didn't scare me. But I do remember feeling intrigued and
horrified. I couldn't understand how the cops could beat
up these people who looked so pretty and so delicate.*

*I didn't understand exactly what was going on,
but I understood that it was important. It helped me
understand that the world was more complicated than I
thought. As a comparison, when I first heard of Martin
Luther King Jr., I was confused, because I thought the
Civil War had ended slavery, and that racism was over*

because of that. This felt similar. I began to understand that people can have different kinds of relationships, like Uncle Ben and Uncle Louie, and that men who loved men and women who loved women were horribly mistreated.

PHOTOGRAPH, PROTESTORS OUTSIDE THE STONEWALL INN

This is one of the most iconic photos of the Stonewall Riots. It was taken by *Village Voice* photographer Fred McDarrah on the second night of the riots. McDarrah and his colleague Lucian Truscott IV rounded up some of the street kids who hung out in Sheridan Square and Christopher Street Park and posed them in front of the Stonewall Inn. The kid on the right, wearing the dark striped shirt, is Thomas Lanigan-Schmidt, who was twenty-one at the time the photo was taken. He is one of the few participants in the riots who is still alive as this book goes to press.

Born in 1948, Thomas grew up poor in Linden, New Jersey. Thomas worked odd jobs to help support his family while attending St. Elizabeth School, where he was constantly bullied by his peers. After finishing high school, he briefly attended the Pratt Institute to study art, then applied to Cooper Union—which promptly rejected his application. "They said something about how they just want you to be *you* when you wrote it—that you should write about who you are," Thomas said in an interview. "But they didn't want me for being me, which was a gay person." To add insult to injury,

97

the admissions office informed Thomas's father about why his son wasn't accepted. "My father ended up going into their office—maybe because they asked for a permanent address in my application materials—and knew about my rejection and why before I did. [It] was extra-horrible for him because he lived in a world where things like [being gay] didn't exist and were terrible. So he basically told me that he knew about my being gay and told me, 'Never tell your mother or your sisters that you're *like that*.'" From that point forward, Thomas lived on the streets of New York City.

Thomas was a semi-regular at the Stonewall Inn. "The place wasn't glamorous," he said in an interview. "The inside was mostly plywood and dark. The best thing in there was the jukebox. The walls were wet in there because the air conditioning didn't work too well. And the place had a kind of stale beer smell going through it." The Friday night before the raid, Thomas had tried to get into the Stonewall Inn, but the guy working the door wouldn't let him. Later, when the raid and subsequent rebellion was underway, Thomas came back to see what was going on—and promptly got into the action. On Saturday night, he and a group of street kids returned and participated in the second night of the uprising—and that's what Fred McDarrah's photo captured.

After the Stonewall Riots, Thomas Lanigan-Schmidt became a successful artist, crafting works out of found and discarded materials. His work has been exhibited throughout the United States and Europe, and his art pieces are represented in the collections of the Metropolitan Museum of Art, the Whitney Museum, and the Museum of Modern Art. He is an instructor at the School of Visual Arts in New York City. Twenty years after the Stonewall Riots, Thomas wrote a piece called "Mother Stonewall and the Golden Rats," which described his recollections of the events of June 28, 1969. Thomas's account captures the essence of what it was like to be a street kid with no money, looking for a place to feel safe and connected to others, and standing up to oppression when there was nothing left for him to lose:

"No, this wasn't a 1960s student riot. Out there were the streets. There were no nice dorms for sleeping. No school cafeteria for certain food. No affluent parents to send us checks. This was a ghetto riot on home turf. We already had our war wounds. This was just another battle. Nobody thought of it as History, Her-Story, My-Story, Your-Story or Our-Story. We were being denied a place to dance together. That's all."

BROKEN JUKEBOX AND VENDING MACHINE INSIDE THE STONEWALL INN

Village Voice photographer Fred McDarrah took most of the iconic photos of the Stonewall Riots. This particular photo is a rare glimpse inside the Stonewall Inn after the riots occurred. On the right is a broken cigarette vending machine. (Back then, most bars and restaurants had them, where people could buy cigarettes by the pack.) On the left is a jukebox that was destroyed after the police freed themselves from inside the bar. If you look in the foreground, you can see one of the records from the jukebox in the trash can, along with beer cans and other garbage. What

you can't see in the photo are the coins, shards of glass, and other items littering the floor, not to mention the smell of old beer, smoke, and garbage. Despite all the damage, the Stonewall Inn reopened the following night, enticing people inside with free sodas.

AFTERMATH

The Stonewall Riots were over. What next? People in the gay community were filled with emotions. They were angry and fired up, without a doubt. Some were in a state of disbelief, not sure what to do next. But running through all of these complicated feelings was a collective sense of euphoria. Everyone seemed to know that the initial seeds of a movement had been planted.

At first, the media coverage of the Stonewall Inn raid

was limited. The *New York Times* ran two stories about it, both of which were buried deep within the Metro section of the paper. If anything, people heard what happened through word of mouth. Craig Rodwell printed up flyers, and a group of activists handed them out to passersby on Saturday morning. Community members, including leaders from the Mattachine Society, posted messages on the boarded-up window of the Stonewall Inn. A few days after the riots, articles finally began appearing in the local papers, first in the *Village Voice*, then in the New York *Daily News*. All of them were highly offensive, turning the whole thing into a big joke. The gay community was infuriated by this, and the jabs from these reporters only fueled their resolve to fight back.

LEAFLET DISTRIBUTED BY CRAIG RODWELL

raig Rodwell was a pro at political organizing. As he witnessed the chaos outside the Stonewall Inn, he knew that this was an opportunity to galvanize the gay community.

The image above is the leaflet Craig and Fred Sargeant distributed in Christopher Street Park and at the Oscar Wilde Memorial Bookshop.

In 1969, there was no email, text messaging, or social media. Passing out leaflets was a way to politicize the public. It was a way to share information, to educate, and to call meetings. "Getting coverage was a challenge," wrote Sargeant in 2009. "The press had a bias against gays then, and it perpetuated the view of Stonewall as the time the drag queens fought back. People were accustomed to getting leaflets, and they would read them. And Craig knew how to write them. It sounds primitive today, but in 1969 it was an effective means of communication."

GET THE MAFIA AND THE COPS OUT OF GAY BARS

The nights of Friday, June 27, 1969 and Saturday, June 28, 1969 will go down in history as the first time that thousands of Homosexual men and women went out into the streets to protest the intolerable situation which has existed in New York City for many years -- namely, the Mafia (or syndicate) control of this city's Gay bars in collusion with certain elements in the Police Dept. of the City of New York. The demonstrations were triggered by a Police raid on the Stonewall Inn late Friday night, June 27th. The purported reason for the raid was the Stonewall's lack of a liquor license. Who's kidding whom? Can anybody really believe that an operation as big as the Stonewall could continue without having a 3 years just a few blocks from the 6th Precinct house without having a liquor license? Ho! The Police have known about the Stonewall operation all along. What has happened is the presence of new "brass" in the 6th Precinct which has vowed to "drive the fags out of the Village."

Many of you have noticed one of the signs which the "management" of the Stonewall has placed outside stating "Legalize Gay bars and lick the problem." This is untrue and they know it. Judge Kenneth Keating (a former U.S. Senator) ruled in January, 1968 that even close dancing between Homosexuals is legal. Since that date there has been nothing illegal, per se, about a Gay bar. What is illegal about New York City's Gay bars today is the Mafia (or syndicate) stranglehold on them. Legitimate Gay businessmen are afraid to open decent Gay bars with a healthy social atmosphere (as opposed to the hell-hole atmosphere of places typified by the Stonewall) because of fear of pressure from the unholy alliance of the Mafia and the elements in the Police Dept. who accept payoffs and protect the Mafia monopoly.

We at the Homophile Youth Movement (HYMN) believe that the only way this monopoly can be broken is through the action of Homosexual men and women themselves. We obviously cannot rely on the various agencies of government who for years have known about this situation but who have refused to do anything about it. Therefore, we urge the following:

1 That Gay businessmen step forward and open Gay bars that will be run legally with competitive pricing and a healthy social atmosphere.

2 That Homosexual men and women boycott places like the Stonewall. The only way, it seems, that we can get criminal elements out of the Gay bars is simply to make it unprofitable for them.

3 That the Homosexual citizens of New York City, and concerned heterosexuals, write to Mayor Lindsay demanding a thorough investigation

NEW YORK TIMES ARTICLE, "4 POLICEMEN HURT IN 'VILLAGE' RAID"

On the first night of the rebellion, Craig Rodwell and his partner Fred Sargeant called the papers, including the *New York Times*, the *New York Post*, and the New York *Daily News*. They knew that what they were witnessing was newsworthy. However, the *New York Times* was the only paper that ran a story the day after the raid happened. The reporter (whose byline wasn't included) stuck to the facts and didn't include any quotes or interviews from people who participated or witnessed the event. The two excerpts below give a sense of how dry the news reporting was:

Hundreds of young men went on a rampage in Greenwich Village shortly after 3 a.m. yesterday after a force of plainclothes men raided a bar that the police said was well known for its homosexual clientele. Thirteen persons were arrested and four policemen injured.

The police estimated that 200 young men had been expelled from the bar. The crowd grew to close to 400 during the melee, which lasted about 45 minutes, they said.

Besides the story being dull and uninspired, it's also notable that it was on page 33—nowhere close to the front page, and easy to miss if you were just browsing the headlines. In fact, an ad for Ohrbach's summer clearance sale dominates the page, dwarfing the story about Stonewall. This wasn't surprising to gay and lesbian people—they were used to being silenced, and it was uncommon for newspapers to print stories about gay people or their rights. But that didn't make it okay for the media to ignore this event.

The next day, June 30, 1969, the *New York Times* printed a follow-up story. Again, there was no byline, the story was buried in the depths of the Metro section of the paper (although this time, the story was on page 22). It's hard to imagine a news story featuring phrases like "heavy police reinforcements," "an inn frequented by homosexuals," and "a crowd of about 400 youths, some of whom were throwing bottles and lighting small fires" being a dry and boring story. But it was—and it was easy to miss the story if you blinked while turning the pages of the *New York Times*. After this, there wouldn't be another story in a mainstream news publication about Stonewall for another week.

4 POLICEMEN HURT IN 'VILLAGE' RAID

Melee Near Sheridan Square
Follows Action at Bar

Hundreds of young men went on a rampage in Greenwich Village shortly after 3 A.M. yesterday after a force of plain-clothes men raided a bar that the police said was well-known for its homosexual clientele. Thirteen persons were arrested and four policemen injured.

The young men threw bricks, bottles, garbage, pennies and a parking meter at the policemen, who had a search warrant authorizing them in investigate reports that liquor was sold illegally at the bar, the Stone-wall Inn, 53 Christopher Street, just off Sheridan Square.

Deputy Inspector Seymour Pine said that a large crowd formed in the square after being evicted from the bar. Police reinforcements were sent to the area to hold off the crowd.

SIGN POSTED OUTSIDE THE STONEWALL INN
BY THE MATTACHINE SOCIETY

On Sunday morning, Dick Leitsch and a group of Mattachine Society members gathered a sheaf of papers, headed for Christopher Street Park, and distributed an article titled "The Hairpin Drop Heard Around the World." Written by Leitsch, who at the time was the president of the New York City chapter of the Mattachine Society, the article referred to Stonewall as "the first gay riots in history" (which was not true), detailing the events that had occurred that previous night. "Hairpin drop" was a subtle slang phrase that referred to gay people. Word traveled fast about what had happened, and a lot of protestors wanted to keep the momentum going.

Members of the Mattachine Society, particularly Dick Leitsch, were feeling nervous. They were used to wearing suits and ties and marching silently, not throwing bottles and fighting against the police. The day after the first night of rioting, the Mattachine Society, in an effort to keep people on their best behavior, posted a sign on the boarded-up window of the Stonewall Inn:

WE HOMOSEXUALS PLEAD WITH OUR PEOPLE TO PLEASE HELP MAINTAIN PEACEFUL AND QUIET CONDUCT ON THE STREETS OF THE VILLAGE—MATTACHINE

While many people weren't interested in maintaining peaceful and quiet conduct, they *were* interested in organizing. Dick and other activists called a meeting of the Mattachine Society to be held on July 9. More than one hundred people showed up. Dick Leitsch stuck to the Mattachine Society script—educate heterosexual people, act respectably, and work toward acceptance, not radicalism. But the group was having none of it. One person proposed the formation of a group called the Gay Liberation Front, and the crowd became electric. That was the death knell of the Mattachine Society, and their last official meeting in New York.

SIGN POSTED OUTSIDE THE STONEWALL INN: "GAY PROHIBITION CORRUPT$ COP$ FEED$ MAFIA"

n the days following the Stonewall rebellion, people filled the boarded-up window of the Stonewall Inn with political messages, announcements, and calls for action. While the previous entry represented the button-up-and-look-good views of the Mattachine Society, this object is reflective of more radical groups. This approach was direct and in-your-face, and they made abundantly clear that they were sick of hiding in the closet, and tired of submitting to the police. It's not known who wrote this message, but whoever it was, that person openly called out the shady relationship between the mob and the cops.

VILLAGE VOICE ARTICLE, "FULL MOON OVER THE STONEWALL"

VILLAGE VOICE ARTICLE, "GAY POWER COMES TO SHERIDAN SQUARE"

Founded in 1955, the *Village Voice* was a weekly newspaper catering to artists, actors, and other creative New Yorkers. Its offices were located at 61 Christopher Street, three doors down from the Stonewall Inn. One of the paper's most popular features was "Scenes," a column that reported the latest cultural shifts. To be mentioned by Howard Smith in "Scenes" in 1969 was the equivalent of a trending tweet in 2019. "Scenes" told Manhattan what was hip, hot, and happening.

In the early morning hours of June 28, 1969, Smith and a colleague named Lucian Truscott IV were writing articles in the *Voice* offices when they heard a commotion outside and looked out the window. "I saw about thirty people in front of the Stonewall," Smith recalled. "I went back to trying to write, looked again, and suddenly there were 100 people. I put on my press card and raced downstairs." Truscott followed him. It was about three a.m.

Once in the street, Smith struck up a conversation with Seymour Pine, deputy inspector of the NYPD's morals squad. Smith flashed his press badge and learned that Pine had begun a raid of the Stonewall Inn without notifying either the Sixth Precinct or the bar owner, which was not the usual practice. The raid had not gone as planned. Only two of the four undercover police had come out of the bar to give the signal to go in. Pine was used to making raids. "All it ever took," recalled Pine, "was going in and saying, 'The place is being raided! Everybody out! And have your IDs ready!' They would show you something, and you'd let them out."

Perhaps it was the full moon. Perhaps it was the heat. Perhaps it was resentment for years of harassment. The patrons in the Stonewall refused to cooperate. "We'd never had resistance before," said Pine. "That night, for some particular reason, they resisted." The police began to arrest any patron who declined to show an ID. "The cops had considerable trouble arresting the few people they wanted to take in for further questioning," said Smith. "Things were already pretty tense. The gay customers freshly ejected from their hangout, prancing high and jubilant in the street, had

the village **VOICE**

15c

New York: 20c elsewhere
© 1969, The Village Voice Inc.   THE WEEKLY NEWSPAPER OF NEW YORK   ● Vol. XIV, No. 38 ● New York, N. Y. ● Thursday, July 3, 1969

Voice: Fred W. McDarrah

IN FRONT OF THE STONEWALL

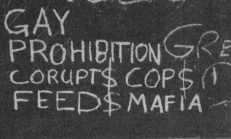

SOME GRAFFITI

Voice: Fred W. McDarrah

Gifted Offenders': I

Completing the Education Of the Black Ex-Convict

by Bell Gale Chevigny

In February, 1967, I was asked to teach an evening class in English composition at Queens College to a group of parolees. They were to be taught under the auspices of the state-supported program for the disadvantaged, SEEK (an acronym for the rather irksome Search for Education, Elevation, and Knowledge), Joseph Mulholland, director of SEEK, which was then half a year old, had been a probation officer and located the students through old associates on the parole board. There would be eight students in their 20s and 30s—all men, all but one black, I was teaching at Sarah Lawrence at the time, and the offer presented an irresistible contrast in every respect, quite apart from the extraordinary personal and vocational challenge it held in itself.

But the challenge took on a shape I had hardly anticipated. The first evening we met I tried to find out where we stood by asking each in turn what he had enjoyed reading. Except for the two who began with magazines and worked their way up to "Marjorie Morningstar" and "The Fountainhead," they had done a good deal of reading in current black literature. Then, when it was his turn, a rangy young man, sprawling over his tiny chair and filling the space around him with expansive gestures, off-handedly listed all of Baldwin and LeRoi Jones, some Genet and Beckett—apologizing parenthetically for not understanding "Watt"—named Celine and Dahlberg, and paused. Before I could respond, a more compact and stationary figure across the room volunteered, "I've read most of that. And Hesse, I liked 'Steppenwolf' especially." The long man straightened slightly in his chair: "I forgot Gertrude Stein—she's the best." "Have you read 'Les Mots' by Sartre?" the other countered, adding softly, "That's 'The Words' in English." "Not yet," the first replied, keeping his cool, "but I read 'Nausea.' " " 'Nausea,' 'Dirty Hands,' 'No Exit,' 'Being and Nothingness'—I guess I've read just about everything of Sartre's," the quiet man

returned. The long body across the room snapped together and whipped around to face him, "Chronologically?" he cried.

The solid fellow replied wryly that he'd read them in the order he'd been able to get hold of them. His name was Arnold Kemp, and from that moment he began more or less to lead the class. (It turned out the lanky admirer of Gertrude Stein was not a parolee and had got into our section by mistake, but he stayed with us, expostulating, to the end.) When asked what he'd like to read, Kemp came up with Nathanael West—"He's really the father of the so-called black humorists." When it came to the vote, although we'd talked about Camus, Faulkner, and Dostoevsky, one after another opted for "that Nathanael West." So dazzled was I that it wasn't until I got home that I realized that most of the class had taken West for a Negro.

It was like that all term. Whenever I tried to find out "where we stood," I risked being thrown off balance by sounding

Continued from page 52

View from Inside

Full Moon Over The Stonewall

by Howard Smith

During the "gay power" riots at the Stonewall last Friday night I found myself on what seemed to me the wrong side of the blue line. Very scary. Very enlightening.

I had struck up a spontaneous relationship with Deputy Inspector Pine, who had marshalled the raid, and was following him closely, listening to all his little dialogues and plans and police inflections. Things were already pretty terse: the gay

customers freshly ejected from their hangout, prancing high and jubilant in the street, had been joined by quantities of Friday night tourists hawking around for Village-type excitement. The cops had considerable trouble arresting the few people they wanted to take in for further questioning. A strange mood was in the crowd—I noticed the full moon. Loud defiances mixed with skittish hilarity made for a more dangerous stage of protest; they

Continued on page 25

View from Outside

Gay Power Comes To Sheridan Square

by Lucian Truscott IV

Sheridan Square this weekend looked like something from a William Burroughs novel as the sudden specter of "gay power" erected its brazen head and spat out a fairy tale the likes of which the area has never seen.

The forces of faggotry, spurred by a Friday night raid on one of the city's largest, most popular, and longest lived gay bars, the Stonewall Inn, rallied Saturday night in an unprecedented protest against the raid and continued Sunday night to assert presence, possibility, and pride until the early hours of Monday morning. "I'm a faggot, and I'm proud of it!" "Gay Power!" "I like boys!"—these and many other slogans were heard all three nights as the show of force by the city's

finery met the force of the city's finest. The result was a kind of liberation, as the gay brigade emerged from the bars, back rooms, and bedrooms of the Village and became street people.

* * *

Cops entered the Stonewall for the second time in a week just before midnight on Friday. It began as a small raid—only two patrolmen, two detectives, and two policewomen were involved. But as the patrons trapped inside were released one by one, a crowd started to gather on the street. It was initially a festive gathering, composed mostly of Stonewall boys who were waiting around for friends still inside or to see what was going to happen. Cheers would go up as favorites would emerge from the door, strike a pose, and swish by the detective with a "Hello there, fella." The stars were in their element. Wrists were limp, hair was primped, and reactions to the applause were classic. "I gave them the gay power bit, and they loved it, girls." "Have you seen Maxine? Where is my wife—I told her not to go far."

Suddenly the paddywagon arrived and the mood of the crowd changed. Three of the more blatant queens—in full drag—were loaded inside, along with the bartender and doorman, to a chorus of catcalls and boos from the crowd. A cry went up to push the paddywagon over, but it drove away before anything could happen. With its exit, the action waned momentarily. The next person to come out was a dyke, and she put up a struggle—from car to door to car again. It was at that

Continued on page 18

been joined by quantities of Friday night tourists hawking around for Village-type excitement. A strange mood was in the crowd."

Robert Bryan was a regular at the Stonewall. "I was on Christopher Street with a friend," recalled Bryan. "Somebody came running down the street and said, 'Go up to Sheridan Square! There's something happening in front of the Stonewall!' There was a lot of excitement. There was a small police van. And there were some drag queens in there. People started jumping on it and bouncing it up and down."

Lured by the noise, more people joined the crowd. "It started to get wilder and bigger," recalled Smith. "Loud defiance mixed with skittish hilarity made for a more dangerous stage of protest." In a few minutes the crowd had swelled to more than four hundred. "People started yelling 'Gay Power!'" said Smith. "They were feeling their impunity. This kind of crowd freaks easily."

Then a lesbian was dragged from the bar and brutally subdued. This set off the crowd. Someone threw a rock at the building. "People started pulling up the stones from around the parking meters, and throwing them," remembered Bryan. "All the windows were immediately broken. We weren't really thinking consciously about what we were doing. We were just reacting, completely emotionally. We were just really frustrated and letting it all out, finally."

The police saw themselves outnumbered and in danger. Pine gathered his men, and they rushed into the bar, bolting the heavy door. Smith was with them. As he and the police watched, the rioters started to break in. "The thumping and shaking of the building was getting stronger and stronger," said Smith. The door didn't hold. "It was a horde of people," said Pine. "They were screaming. They were throwing bottles. They were throwing coins. And that's where this guy flipped this coin and got a cop in the eye." The sight of blood had an effect. "Everyone went crazy," said Smith. "The police went crazy." The trapped police were on the verge of using guns, but Pine managed to keep them in line, even as windows were breaking. At one point someone poured lighter fluid through a crack in the door and tried to start a fire. As if on cue, the Tactical Patrol Force arrived, wearing face-concealing helmets and carrying clubs. The fire was extinguished, and the police trapped inside the Stonewall were released.

On Saturday night, less than twenty-four hours after the bar had been raided, another crowd gathered. Again the Tactical Patrol Force arrived. The NYPD obviously regarded the unrest as a major situation. Likewise, the crowds milling on Christopher Street looked on the police as a fascist intrusion. The force began herding the crowd down the street, moving westward, but at the corner of Waverly Place there was a standoff.

The tension was momentarily eased by some spontaneous theatricality. A group of gay men lined up in front of the phalanx of police and began doing high kicks à la the Rockettes of Radio City Music Hall. Realizing that they were being ridiculed, the police began to advance, forcing the gays down Christopher to Seventh Avenue and then securing the area at both entrances. The violence was limited to minor injuries, and there were only a few arrests, but the point had been made: The insurrection of the first night was not an isolated incident.

Accordingly, the TPF made another sweep on Sunday night. Lucian Truscott IV, covering the event, ran into Allen Ginsberg, who was a poet, writer, and for two decades a leading countercultural figure. "Gay Power!" said Ginsberg. "Isn't that great! We're one of the largest minorities in the country, ten percent, you know. It's about time we did something to assert ourselves." Ginsberg told Truscott that he was impressed by the look of the Stonewall rioters. "The guys there were so beautiful. They've lost that wounded look that fags all had ten years ago." Truscott was perplexed by Ginsberg's attitude. "As Ginsberg turned to head home," wrote Truscott, "he waved and yelled, 'Defend the fairies!' and bounced on across the square. He enjoyed the prospect of 'gay power' and is probably working on a manifesto for the movement right now. Watch out. The liberation is under way."

While the *Village Voice* of today is supportive of the gay community, in 1969 it was anti-homosexual. "Sheridan Square this weekend," wrote Truscott, "looked like something from a William Burroughs novel as the sudden specter of 'gay power' erected its brazen head and spat out a fairy tale the likes of which the area has never seen. The forces of faggotry, spurred by a Friday night raid on one of the city's largest, most popular and longest-lived gay bars, rallied Saturday night in an unprecedented protest against the raid and continued Sunday night to assert presence, possibility, and pride."

A "fairy tale"? The "faggotry"? These were not words that gay people used to describe themselves or their community. The newspaper referred to the Stonewall Riots as "the Great Faggot Rebellion." Both Smith and Truscott used slurs like "dyke" and "faggot," littering their articles with stereotypes about gay people. "The stars were in their element," wrote Truscott. "Wrists were limp, hair was primped, and reactions to applause were classic: 'I gave them the gay power bit, and they loved it, girls.'" Truscott was trying to reduce the gay community to a ghetto of effeminates, even referring to the protestors as "fags." Maybe he thought this was funny. To the gay community it was no joke.

On the day these articles were published, a crowd of angry protestors marched down Christopher Street to the *Village Voice*'s offices, threatening to burn them down. Once more, the Tactical Patrol Force showed up, and a street fight ensued between police and demonstrators. Shops were looted, scores of people were injured, and five people were arrested.

For years the gay community had been deprived of its rights. On June 28, it had been provoked. Now it was ready to fight. "I knew within a month," recalled Howard Smith, "that this was important—in a cultural sense. I could see the difference in the militancy of people from the gay community."

PHOTOGRAPH, WOMEN HOLDING HANDS, 1969 ANNUAL REMINDER

July 4, 1969, the date of the Annual Reminder in Philadelphia, was a few days after the Stonewall Riots. After Stonewall, which was an explosive act of resistance compared to the silent pickets of the Mattachine Society, some activists felt that the Annual Reminder had run its course. For starters, many gay activists didn't want to wear such traditional clothing and picket silently. They wanted to speak up, stand up for themselves, and demand their rights. Ultimately, they decided to go forward with the Annual Reminder, and they reluctantly agreed to follow the dress code and remain silent during the picket. However, there was much more tension, anger, and energy at that year's Annual Reminder compared to years past—and there was greater potential for a more drastic act of resistance.

For a time, protestors followed their marching orders—they stayed silent and held their signs high, wearing their suits and dresses. But then, at one point during the protest, two women stepped out of the single-file line and held hands—which was a violation of the Mattachine Society's

demonstration guidelines. Frank Kameny, who was partic-
ipating in the Annual Reminder, was furious, and he headed
over to the two women and tried to break them up. The two
women refused, and Craig Rodwell, who was also in attendance, raised his voice and publicly criticized Kameny to
members of the press who were there. That was the last year
the Annual Reminder was held—another nail in the coffin
for the Mattachine Society and their efforts to quietly blend
into mainstream society.

NEW YORK *DAILY NEWS* ARTICLE, "HOMO NEST RAIDED, QUEEN BEES ARE STINGING MAD"

The New York *Daily News* ran an article about Stonewall on June 29, 1969—the same day the *New York Times* published its first article. Titled "3 Cops Hurt as Bar Raid Riles Crowd," the story, buried on page 30, was clearly biased toward the police. After that, the *Daily News* went silent until July 9, when the newspaper finally published a second, more extensive article. This article was more detailed, and compared to the two *New York Times* stories, it was anything but boring. But it was also anything but respectful.

"Last weekend the queens had turned commando and stood bra strap to bra strap against an invasion of the helmeted Tactical Patrol Force," wrote Jerry Lisker. "Queen Power reared its bleached blonde head in revolt. New York City experienced its first homosexual riot. Queens, princesses, and ladies-in-waiting began hurling anything they could lay their polished, manicured finger nails on. Bobby pins, compacts, curlers, lipstick tubes, and other femme fatale missiles were flying in the direction of the cops. The war was on. The lilies of the valley had become carnivorous jungle plants."

Instead of writing a legitimate news story, journalist Jerry Lisker chose to insult, degrade, and dehumanize the gay community—particularly any form of feminine expression—and treat the fight for gay liberation as a joke. It was an incredibly offensive article, even back in 1969. Unlike previous stories, this July 9 article wasn't buried or hidden at all; in fact, the headline was brandished across the front page and "above the fold" (meaning the top half of the newspaper, above where it was folded in half). The gay community was infuriated by the tone of the article, fostering even more distrust toward the mainstream media.

LIBERATION

After the Annual Reminder, it was clear that the gay community was ready for a new form of activism. People didn't want to act demure and quietly hold signs anymore. They wanted to capitalize on the momentum of the Stonewall Riots and do what other social movements had been doing for some time. They wanted to march, demonstrate, sit in, and speak out. The riots had simmered down, but the collective anger of the gay community had reached a boiling point. They wanted to stand up and fight for their rights. Members of the Mattachine Society tried to organize people, but activists were fed up with their cautious, well-dressed, and well-groomed approach. In the months after the Stonewall Riots, the Mattachine Society was laid to rest, and activists formed new, more revolutionary organizations.

GAY LIBERATION FRONT (GLF) POSTER

The anger at the Mattachine Society's cautious approach came to a head at their next meeting, held on July 9. Dick Leitsch, who led the meeting, tried in vain to convince the group that throwing bottles and marching in the streets wasn't going to accomplish anything. But the activists didn't want to tone it down. That night, the Mattachine Society took its final breaths, and a new group was born: the Gay Liberation Front (GLF).

The GLF wasn't a single-issue group; in addition to fighting for gay rights, they opposed other social inequities such as racism, class oppression, sexism, and oppression of Third World countries. Many of their members were also active in the antiwar movement, and the group actively supported the Black Panther Party, a radical organization that fought for the rights of African American people. The GLF organized protests, marches, sit-ins, and other political activities. Compared to the Mattachine Society, the GLF was beyond radical.

That didn't mean the group didn't have its struggles. Some people felt that the group was *too* radical. Others were concerned that their political platform was too broad and that it watered down the focus on gay liberation. People who were dissatisfied with the GLF started forming their own groups, such as the Gay Activists Alliance (GAA), the Lavender Menace and Radicalesbians, and Street Transvestite Action Revolutionaries (STAR). By 1972, the infighting within the main group had come to a breaking point, and that year GLF officially shuttered their operations.

GAY ACTIVISTS ALLIANCE (GAA) POLITICAL PATCH

B y the fall of 1969, some GLF members were unhappy with the way the group was being run. At least four members—Arthur Evans, Jim Owles, Arthur Bell, and Marty Robinson—began talking about breaking away and forming their own group. On December 21, 1969, a group of about twenty people met at Arthur Bell's apartment, and together they formed the Gay Activists Alliance (GAA). Unlike the GLF, which focused on a wide range of social injustices, the GAA focused solely on gay and lesbian rights. They were more formally organized than the GLF, using *Robert's Rules of Order* and parliamentary procedure to run meetings. In 1971, the group rented a firehouse in New York City's SoHo neighborhood, and the Firehouse became the GAA's headquarters. One of GAA's members, Tom Doerr, was a graphic designer, and he created the GAA's logo—a lowercase Greek letter lambda (Λ), which symbolizes many things. In Greek culture, the lambda symbolized balance; for the Spartans, it represented

127

unity; and the Romans believed that it reflected the light of knowledge. Modern physicists use the lambda to represent a change in energy—which, in a sense, is what the GAA was working toward.

Compared to the GLF, the GAA used more conventional methods to achieve change. They fought to overturn discriminatory laws, and they worked to hold politicians accountable to the gay community. However, the GAA is probably best known for the zap—a direct confrontation with a public figure regarding LGBT rights, designed to embarrass a political figure or celebrity and gain media attention. One of GAA's early zaps targeted New York City mayor John Lindsay, who refused to meet with the GAA and take an active stance on gay rights issues, largely because he feared it would hurt his political career. The GAA responded by "zapping" him. On opening night of the 1970 Metropolitan Opera season, members of the GAA infiltrated the opera house and shouted gay rights chants as Lindsay and his wife entered the building.

Seeing how effective the GAA was at getting people's attention, other gay activist groups began to use this political tactic. Activist Mark Segal, who witnessed the raid and uprising at the Stonewall Inn, became known for his television zaps. Some of his targets included *The Tonight Show*

Starring Johnny Carson and *The Mike Douglas Show*. His most famous zap took place on December 11, 1973, on *CBS Evening News with Walter Cronkite*. Mark and a friend lied their way into the CBS television studio, and while Walter Cronkite was anchoring the broadcast, Mark ran in front of the television camera holding a sign that said GAYS PROTEST CBS PREJUDICE. Walter Cronkite kept his composure, and later met with Mark Segal and arranged meetings with top management to discuss news coverage of gay issues. The zap—and the resulting meetings—were effective; on May 6, 1974, *CBS Evening News with Walter Cronkite* broadcast a news segment about gay rights.

Over the years, a number of spin-off groups formed from the main GAA organization. The most well-known of those groups, formed in 1973, was the National Gay Task Force—now the National LGBTQ Task Force. While the GAA was a central organization in the gay rights movement for many years, it eventually folded in 1981.

ORNAMENTAL IRON FENCE, GREENWICH VILLAGE, NEW YORK CITY

New York City, particularly Greenwich Village, is filled with ornamental iron. The fire escapes of apartment buildings, like the one Margot Avery watched the riots from, are made of ornamental iron. So are gates, entryways, window security bars, and balconies. Christopher Street Park is surrounded by an ornamental iron fence, with spikes at the top. In 1970, so was the NYPD Sixth Precinct building—as Diego Viñales discovered.

Viñales was born in Buenos Aires, Argentina, probably in 1946 or 1947, and spent his childhood in a *villa miseria*—a poor village—outside of the city. The houses were made out of scraps of wood and corrugated tin. There was no plumbing, and water had to be carried in buckets by hand. Viñales's family had no money, and he left school at the age of twelve so he could work. When he was in his early twenties, Viñales met an American man named Jim who lived in New York City. Jim encouraged him to go to school in the United States, and he helped Viñales get a student visa. When Jim returned to New York, Viñales came with him, and they lived together

in Jim's apartment in the West Village. But Viñales, filled with excitement about living in New York City, put off going to school, and eventually his student visa expired. And then the Snake Pit happened.

The Snake Pit was a gay bar located at 213 West 10th Street, in the basement of an apartment building. Like the Stonewall Inn, the Snake Pit operated illegally as an after-hours club, and it attracted people who weren't welcome in other establishments. Early in the morning of March 8, 1970, Inspector Seymour Pine (of Stonewall Inn fame) conducted a raid on the Snake Pit. Raids of gay bars didn't stop after Stonewall, although police now realized that anytime a gay bar was raided, riots were a distinct possibility. In order to prevent that from happening, Pine took charge from the start, arresting 167 people and booking them at the Sixth Precinct. Diego Viñales was one of those who was arrested that night.

Viñales was very scared. He knew his student visa had expired and that he could be deported back to Argentina. Additionally, his English was not very good, and he didn't understand everything that was going on, or what was being said to him. Panicked and hoping to escape, Viñales leapt out of a second-story window at the Sixth Precinct, and he impaled himself on the wrought-iron fence that surrounded the property. When rescuers arrived on the scene, they had to cut the fence in order to get Viñales off, and he was taken to the hospital with a piece of the fence still in his body.

Word got around quickly that the Snake Pit had been raided, and that one of the bar patrons was seriously injured from jumping out a Sixth Precinct window. Although Viñales was in stable condition at St. Vincent's Hospital, the word on the street was that he was dead or was dying. In response, the Gay Activists Alliance and Gay Liberation Front quickly assembled a protest. About five hundred people marched from Christopher Street Park to the police station, and another group of people led a candlelight vigil at St. Vincent's Hospital. By this time, gay rights organizations had begun to gain strength, and they were able to organize and act quickly in response to injustices committed against their community. These protests helped spark interest in the upcoming Christopher Street Liberation Day events already planned for June 28, 1970.

Viñales survived the fall, but nothing more is known about him.

RITA MAE BROWN'S LAVENDER MENACE T-SHIRT

T he names people typically associate with Stonewall are Craig Rodwell, Dick Leitsch, Thomas Lanigan-Schmidt, Marsha P. Johnson, Bob Kohler, and Sylvia Rivera—to name a few. But what about lesbian women? Other than the unidentified Stonewall Lesbian, were any lesbian women even there?

The short answer to that question is yes. The longer answer is more complicated. Most of the people who have come forward and shared their accounts are men. The most active gay organization in town was the Mattachine Society, and it was for men. By 1969, the Daughters of Bilitis was all but dead; only two dozen people had attended their annual convention that prior year, and most younger women were flocking to the feminist movement. Unfortunately, neither the male-dominated gay liberation movement nor the feminist movement were very welcoming of lesbian women. Betty Friedan, author of the groundbreaking book *The Feminine Mystique* and founder of the National Organization for Women (NOW), famously referred to lesbians as a "lavender menace" that could take down the whole movement. And

Rita Mae Brown wearing the Lavender Menace T-shirt;
others unidentified

groups like the Gay Liberation Front allowed women to participate but weren't always willing to address their issues.

Rita Mae Brown, a lesbian who also identified as a feminist, had difficulty finding a group that addressed all aspects
of her identity. She took a job with NOW as an administrative
assistant but quit in January 1970 after Betty Friedan made
her "lavender menace" comment. Then she joined a group
called Redstockings, which was more radical than NOW, but
still didn't really address lesbian issues. The last straw was

when Rita saw the conference schedule for NOW's Second Congress to Unite Women, which didn't include lesbians in any of their programming. Infuriated, she decided to take action and form her own lesbian-feminist group.

Rita attended a meeting of the Gay Liberation Front and convinced the women there that they needed their own organization. This new group called themselves the Lavender Menace, and their first direct action was a zap against NOW's planned Congress. They met at the apartment of Ellen Broidy and Linda Rhodes, used their bathroom to dye two dozen shirts lavender, then silk-screened the words LAVENDER MENACE on them. They created a manifesto called "The Woman-Identified Woman," authored under the collective pseudonym "Radicalesbians," that called for a unique lesbian feminist voice in the women's movement. They also made signs bearing slogans such as "You're Going to Love the Lavender Menace" and "Women's Liberation IS a Lesbian Plot."

In her memoir, *Tales of the Lavender Menace*, founding member Karla Jay describes what happened:

> *Finally, we were ready. The Second Congress to*
> *Unite Women got under way on May 1 at 7:00 p.m. at*
> *Intermediate School 70 on West Seventeenth Street in*

Manhattan. About three hundred women filed into the school auditorium. Just as the first speaker came to the microphone, Jesse Falstein, a GLF member, and Michela [Griffo] switched off the lights and pulled the plug on the mike. (They had cased the place the previous day, and knew exactly where the switches were and how to work them.) I was planted in the middle of the audience, and I could hear my coconspirators running down both aisles. Some were laughing, while others were emitting rebel yells. When Michela and Jesse flipped the lights back on, both aisles were lined with seventeen lesbians wearing their Lavender Menace T-shirts and holding the placards we had made. Some invited the audience to join them. I stood up and yelled, "Yes, yes, sisters! I'm tired of being in the closet because of the women's movement." Much to the horror of the audience, I unbuttoned the long-sleeved red blouse I was wearing and ripped it off. Underneath, I was wearing a Lavender Menace T-shirt. There were hoots of laughter as I joined the others in the aisles. Then Rita [Mae Brown] yelled to members of the audience, "Who wants to join us?"

"I do, I do," several replied.

Then Rita also pulled off her Lavender Menace

T-shirt. Again, there were gasps, but underneath she had on another one. More laughter. The audience was on our side.

After the zap, members of the Lavender Menace distributed copies of "The Woman-Identified Woman," which eventually became the founding document for the Radicalesbians, a group that formed after the zap to continue their activism. In September 1971, at NOW's national conference, delegates passed a resolution affirming lesbianism and lesbian rights as "a legitimate concern for feminism."

Both the Lavender Menace and Radicalesbians were the launching point for a national lesbian-feminist movement. Meanwhile, Rita Mae Brown continued to be politically active while going to school and earning a bachelor's degree in classics, then two doctoral degrees, one in literature, the other in political science. Rita Mae Brown is probably best known for her bestselling books, including the lesbian classic *Rubyfruit Jungle*, as well as her Mrs. Murphy Mystery series, authored with her cat, Sneaky Pie Brown.

CHRISTOPHER STREET LIBERATION DAY MARCH ADVERTISEMENT

Planning for the July Fourth Annual Reminder protest at Independence Hall usually began the previous fall. They needed to raise money, advertise the event, arrange transportation, contact the media, and take care of other logistics. But activists weren't eager to march silently wearing suits and dresses. It was time for a more radical action.

Craig Rodwell had an idea. What if, instead of the Annual Reminder, they organized a march to commemorate the anniversary of the raids at the Stonewall Inn? He shared the idea with his partner, Fred Sargeant, and their friends Ellen Broidy and Linda Rhodes. Together, they drafted a proposal, and on November 2, 1969, Ellen Broidy presented a resolution to the next Eastern Regional Conference of Homophile Organizations (ERCHO), which was the group that had orchestrated the Annual Reminders. This was the proposal:

That the Annual Reminder, in order to be more relevant,
reach a greater number of people, and encompass the
ideas and ideals of the larger struggle in which we are

engaged—that of our fundamental human rights—be
moved both in time and location.

We propose that a demonstration be held annually
on the last Saturday in June in New York City to
commemorate the 1969 spontaneous demonstrations
on Christopher Street and this demonstration be called
CHRISTOPHER STREET LIBERATION DAY. No dress
or age regulations shall be made for this demonstration.

We also propose that we contact Homophile
organizations throughout the country and suggest
that they hold parallel demonstrations on that day. We
propose a nationwide show of support.

The resolution passed unanimously.

Starting in January, Rodwell, Sargeant, Broidy, and
Rhodes began holding regular meetings at Rodwell's apartment at 350 Bleecker Street, a few blocks from the Stonewall
Inn. They got representatives from the other gay organizations to join them, including Brenda Howard from the Gay
Liberation Front and Foster Gunnison from the Mattachine Society. Gunnison handled the national fundraising
effort, reaching out to gay organizations across the country.
Howard solicited donations via the Gay Liberation Front,

and Sargeant collected donations at the Oscar Wilde Memorial Bookshop. Although the original resolution called for the event to be held on the last Saturday in June, the march was ultimately scheduled for Sunday, June 28, 1970, exactly one year after the Stonewall Inn had been raided.

This advertisement was posted widely in Greenwich Village, and distributed at the Oscar Wilde Memorial Bookshop. Broidy, Rhodes, Howard, and Judy Miller handled the advertising and distribution of flyers and information, as well as other miscellaneous tasks.

PHOTOGRAPH, BRENDA HOWARD WITH PROTEST SIGN

O rganizing marches and protests is hard work. Pulling it off takes blood, sweat, and tears—and often the people behind the scenes don't get credit for their efforts. Brenda Howard (at far left in the photograph on page 144) is one of those people—a workhorse for the gay liberation movement, and an activist in her own right.

A lifelong political agitator, Howard was born in the Bronx and grew up on Long Island. She was active in the antiwar movement, and for a time lived in an urban commune with other antiwar activists. Frustrated by sexism within that movement, she joined the feminist movement and advocated for women's rights. Then Stonewall happened—and that's what started her lifelong work with the LGBT community.

After the riots, Howard joined the Gay Liberation Front (GLF), and served as the liaison between the GLF and the Christopher Street Liberation Day Committee (CSLDC). She was also a member of the Gay Activists Alliance (GAA), chairing their Speakers Bureau for many years. A "workaholic for the movement," Howard was willing to do all sorts of tasks, including making phone calls, distributing flyers, and raising money. It was she who suggested that the CSLDC plan a weeklong series of events leading up to the march. And she was the first person to refer to the march as Pride.

Brenda Howard was openly bisexual and polyamorous (loving more than one person at a time), a rarity in the 1970s, and an identity that wasn't well understood or accepted. Most of Howard's activism throughout her life focused on the bisexual community. In 1988, she cofounded the New York Area Bisexual Network, which was an information clearinghouse for bisexual and bi-friendly organizations in the greater New York area. A few years later, she successfully advocated for the inclusion of bisexuals in the 1993 March on Washington. She's been referred to as an "in-your-face" activist, fighting for "anyone who had their rights trampled on." Howard isn't one of the more well-known activists in the gay liberation movement, but in many ways, she's the reason why we have Pride celebrations today.

MAP OF THE CHRISTOPHER STREET LIBERATION DAY MARCH ROUTE

This map details the exact route of the Christopher Street Liberation Day march. A few dozen participants gathered at Sheridan Square, went up Waverly Place and Washington Street, then turned left onto Sixth Avenue. As they marched, more people joined them along the parade route, and by the time they reached Sheep Meadow in Central Park, there were more than two thousand people.

Along the three-and-a-half-mile route, marchers passed by a number of iconic New York sites of interest, including Macy's and Herald Square at 34th Street; Bryant Park and the New York Public Library, between West 40th and 42nd Streets; and Radio City Music Hall, at the corner of West 50th Street. Imagine—just a few years earlier, gay and lesbian people stayed in hiding. When they socialized in public places, they used pseudonyms to enter bars and clubs and on homophile membership lists. Not this time. They took to the streets, and they were out, loud, and proud, all the way from Sheridan Square to Central Park, on one of the most well-traveled streets in New York City.

STAGING AREA: NUMBERS IN SHADED AREAS INDICATE ORDER OF
PROCESSION INTO MARCH.   ARROWS INDICATE DIRECTION OF
MARCH FROM STAGING AREAS INTO SIXTH AVENUE.
⌷ INDICATES SUBWAY ENTRANCE.
WPH INDICATES PUBLIC TELEPHONE.
WRH INDICATES RESTAURANT WHICH MAY HAVE TOILET FACILITIES

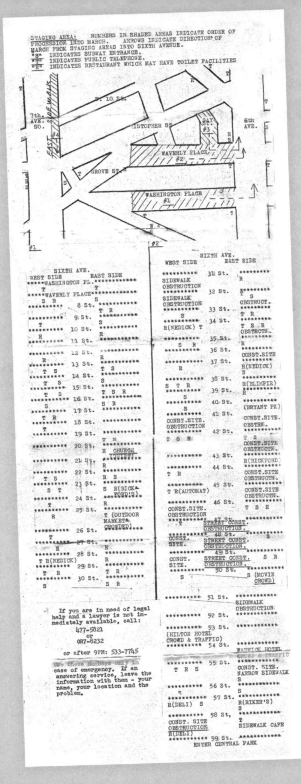

If you are in need of legal
help and a lawyer is not immediately available, call:
477-5821
or
OR7-8232

or after 9PM: 533-7745

Use these numbers only in
case of emergency. If an
answering service, leave the
information with them - your
name, your location and the
problem.

SIXTH AVE.

WEST SIDE		EAST SIDE
********WASHINGTON PL.*********		
T		R
********WAVERLY PLACE********		
S R		S
*********	8 St.	*********
		T R
*********	9 St.	*********
		S
T	10 St.	R
R		
*********	11 St.	*********
*********	12 St.	*********
R		R
T S	13 St.	T S
*********	14 St.	S
T S	15 St.	R
T S	16 St.	S R
*********	17 St.	*********
T R	18 St.	
T	19 St.	*********
*********	20 St.	T N
		R CHURCH (QUIET)
*********	21 St.	*********
*********	22 St.	R
T S	23 St.	S
S T		S R(BICK-
	24 St.	FORD'S)
T	25 St.	R
R		T (OUTDOOR MARKET CROWDED)
*********	26 St.	T
********* 27 St.		*********
R		R
R(NEDICK)	28 St.	R
*********	29 St.	*********
T R	30 St.	T R
S		S R

SIXTH AVE.

WEST SIDE		EAST SIDE
	31 St.	R
SIDEWALK OBSTRUCTION		
*********	32 St.	T S
SIDEWALK OBSTRUCTION		T OBSTRUCT.
*********	33 St.	*********
S		T R
*********	34 St.	*********
R(NEDICK) T		T S R OBSTRCTN.
*********	35 St.	*********
S R		*********
*********	36 St.	CONST.SITE
		R(NEDICK)
*********	37 St.	S
R		*********
*********	38 St.	R(ELIE PIE)
S T R	39 St.	R
S		*********
*********	40 St.	(BRYANT PK.)
*********	41 St.	CONST.SITE
CONST.SITE. OBSTRUCTION		OBSTRN.
*********	42 St.	*********
T S R		T S CONST.SITE OBSTRUCTN.
*********	43 St.	*********
		R(BICKFORD)
*********	44 St.	CONST.SITE OBSTRUCTN.
T R		*********
*********	45 St.	CONST.SITE OBSTRUCTN.
T R(AUTOMAT)		*********
*********	46 St.	T S R
CONST.SITE. OBSTRUCTION		*********
T	47 St.	S
STREET CONST. OBSTRUCTION.		*********
*********	48 St.	*********
CONST. SITE.	STREET CONST. OBSTRUCTION.	S
*********	49 St.	*********
CONST. SITE.	STREET CONST. OBSTRUCTION.	S R
*********	50 St.	*********
S		S (MOVIE CROWD)
*********	51 St.	*********
		SIDEWALK OBSTRUCTION
*********	52 St.	*********
*********	53 St.	*********
(HILTON HOTEL CROWD & TRAFFIC)		
*********	54 St.	*********
		WARWICK HOTEL CROWD & TRAFFIC
*********	55 St.	CONST. SITE. NARROW SIDEWALK
T R S		S
*********	56 St.	S
S		*********
*********	57 St.	R(RIKER'S)
R(DELI) S		*********
*********	58 St.	T
CONST. SITE OBSTRUCTION		SIDEWALK CAFE
R(DELI)		
*********	59 St.	*********
ENTER CENTRAL PARK		

FRED SARGEANT'S BULLHORN

CSLD ARMBAND

Fred Sargeant, Craig Rodwell's partner, was the only person at the march with a bullhorn. He led the chants throughout the entire march. In this image, Fred is on the left, holding the bullhorn. Both he and Craig wore orange armbands with the initials CSLD on them. The bright orange armbands helped marchers identify the organizers of the march. All of them were aware of their rights, and they knew what to do if someone was arrested or if they were otherwise harassed by the police. Of course, none of the organizers anticipated that the crowd would swell to more than two thousand participants. The march and gay be-in in Central Park was peaceful, and the police did not intervene.

The armband in the photo belonged to Craig Rodwell. It is now housed at the New York Public Library.

Fred Sargeant (LEFT) and Craig Rodwell

STREET TRANSVESTITE ACTION REVOLUTIONARIES BANNER

The evening of the march, the Gay Activists Alliance hosted a dance in the basement of Weinstein Hall, a New York University dormitory located near Washington Square Park. At the time, other than seedy bars like the Stonewall Inn, there weren't many social spaces for gay

Sylvia Rivera (SECOND FROM LEFT); others unidentified

and lesbian people, and gay youth and young adults were hungry for a place to meet and hang out. The dance was very successful, and members of the Christopher Street Liberation Day Committee (CSLDC), who organized the march and be-in held earlier that day, decided to coordinate a series of four additional dances to be held at Weinstein Hall. The Dance-a-Fairs, which would raise money for services for the gay community, were scheduled for four Friday evenings in August and September.

The first two Dance-a-Fairs went smoothly. However, claiming concerns about the impact of these dances on their young and impressionable first-year college students, university officials canceled the remaining two dances. The CSLDC convinced the NYU administration to hold the third dance, scheduled for August 28, 1970. However, as the fall semester approached, the university banned all gay social functions, including that third dance, until they could convene a group of psychologists and clergy to determine whether homosexuality was "morally acceptable."

The gay community wasn't going to let this go. In September of 1970, members of the NYU Gay Student Liberation group held a five-day sit-in at New York University's Weinstein Hall. The student group called upon the Gay Liberation

Front for reinforcements, and within a few hours there were about seventy people, including activists Marsha P. Johnson and Sylvia Rivera, occupying the building. During those five days, activists picketed, distributed flyers, held teach-ins on gay liberation, and organized meetings with students who lived in the dorm. The administration used every tactic they could think of to get them to leave, including "freezing" the building by turning up the air conditioner. By the end of the protest, students decided to organize a dance at NYU's Weinstein Hall, without getting university permission, to be held on Friday, September 25, 1970.

The afternoon of the dance, NYU officials called New York City's Tactical Patrol Force, and when they arrived, they barricaded all of the doors except one and gave activists ten seconds to leave. Sylvia Rivera was among those who refused, and she was carried out by the police. This led to a series of demonstrations held in Greenwich Village against the university and at the NYU Student Center. Activists also staged demonstrations at NYU's Bellevue Hospital, where doctors treated homosexuality by using shock therapy.

A number of the participants at the Weinstein Hall occupation were women, people of color, and drag queens, most of whom felt marginalized within the larger gay rights movement. In the aftermath of the Weinstein Hall occupation, Sylvia Rivera and Marsha P. Johnson formed a new organization called Street Transvestite Action Revolutionaries (STAR), which would help youth struggling with their sexual identity find housing and food, as well as get legal and emotional support. "STAR was for the street gay people, the street homeless people and anybody that needed help at that time," Sylvia said in an interview. "Marsha and I had always sneaked people into our hotel rooms. Marsha and I decided to get a building. We were trying to get away from the Mafia's control at the bars."

In November of 1970, Sylvia and Marsha opened STAR House, which over the next few years would have many incarnations. The first was an abandoned trailer located in a Greenwich Village parking lot. When the trailer was moved by the city, they found a four-bedroom apartment in a building located at 213 East 2nd Street. There was no electricity, and the heating and plumbing were unreliable, but the rundown apartment was a safe haven for youth. This STAR House operated until July of 1971, when the landlord evicted the residents, claiming they hadn't paid their rent. Sylvia and Marsha continued to advocate for their community throughout their lives.

PHOTOGRAPH, SYLVIA RIVERA
AT THE 1973 CHRISTOPHER STREET LIBERATION DAY MARCH

After 1970, the Christopher Street Liberation Day parade and rally became an annual event. But it wasn't all sparkles and rainbows. By 1973, conflicts between lesbians, gay men, and drag queens were heating up. Gay men dominated the social and political scene, and lesbians and drag queens felt left out, ignored, and marginalized by their own community. Additionally, there were rifts between lesbians and drag queens, with some lesbian feminists believing that drag queens were threatening their hard work, mimicking patriarchal expectations of how women should look, dress, and act. All of this came to a head at the 1973 Christopher Street Liberation Day parade, when Sylvia Rivera attempted to step up to the microphone to speak. Gay participants tried to block her, but she managed to get onto the stage and take the microphone. Here's a transcript of her famous "Y'all Better Quiet Down" speech:

> *Y'all better quiet down! I've been trying to get up here ALL day for your gay brothers and your gay sisters in jail! That*

Sylvia Rivera (LEFT); others unidentified

[sic] *write me every ******* week and ask for help, and you all don't do a ******* thing for them. Have you ever been beaten up? And raped? And jailed? Now think about it, they've been beaten up and raped and so they have to spend much of their money in jail to get their self home and try to get their sex change. The women have tried to fight*

for their sex changes, or to become women, of the women's liberation. And they write to STAR, not the women's group. They do not write women. They do not write men. They write to STAR, because we've been trying to do something for them. I have been to jail. I have been raped, and beaten, many times! By men! Heterosexual men, that do not belong in the homosexual shelter. But do you do anything for them? No! You all tell me to go hide my tail between my legs. I will not no longer put up with this ****. I have been beaten, I have had my nose broken, I have been thrown in jail, I have lost my job, I have lost my apartment, for gay liberation. And you all treat me this way? What the ****'s wrong with you all? Think about that! I do not believe in a revolution, but you all do. I believe in the gay power. I believe in us getting our rights or else I would not be out there fighting for our rights. That's all I wanted to say to you all people. If you all want to know about the people that are in jail, and do not forget Bambi L'Amour, Andora Marks, Kenny Messner, and other gay people are in jail, come and see the people at STAR House on 12th Street, on 640 12th Street, between B and C, Apartment 14. The people there are trying to do something for ALL of us, and not men and women that belong to a White middle-class

White club! And that's what you all belong to! Revolution
NOWWWWW!!! Gimme a "G"! Gimme an "A"! Gimme
a "Y"! Gimme a "P"! Gimme an "O"! Gimme a "W"!
Gimme an "E"! Gimme an "R"! Gay... GAY POWER!!
LOUDER—GAY POWER!

Sylvia's words were like a shot of reality to the gay community. She knew what it was like to be homeless and without food, and with no place to go. She also knew what it was like to be beaten up and abused, just because people felt threatened by her gender presentation. For the rest of her life, Sylvia Rivera was a powerful advocate for the most disenfranchised members of the community. However, her words didn't register immediately with the gay community. It would take at least two more decades before the rights she fought for, which came to be part of the transgender rights movement, gained significant traction.

EPILOGUE

The Stonewall Inn and Christopher Street Park will always be iconic to the LGBT community. They're not only important sites of resistance, but they occupy a unique place in our history. Because of Stonewall and the gay liberation movement that followed, LGBT people are more visible and powerful than ever before. Pride celebrations are held throughout the world, and crowds of people fill the streets. Movies and television shows feature LGBT characters. And same-sex couples can get married, and their marriages are recognized by the federal government. Compare that to the 1950s, when gay and lesbian people could get thrown in jail, lose their jobs or housing, be subjected to inhumane psychiatric treatment, and be treated as degenerate lowlifes in society.

However, the movement is far from over. While the Stonewall Riots serve as an important symbol of how far the LGBT community has come, they also remind us of the dangers of complacency. There are, for example, no federal employment protections for LGBT people; it's perfectly legal in some states to fire someone (or refuse to hire them) simply because they're lesbian, gay, bisexual, or transgender. The federal Fair Housing Act does not protect people from housing discrimination on the basis of sexual orientation or gender identity. In many states, youth under the age of eighteen can be subjected by their parents to conversion therapy to change their sexual orientation or gender identity. Transgender people routinely face discrimination in health care, employment, and housing. The bathroom wars rage on in schools and public facilities: Some states have passed laws restricting access to gendered bathrooms, while other states have legislated broader access for transgender people. People of color also experience marginalization within the LGBT community, an ongoing problem still to be addressed.

Think of all of the people involved in the Stonewall Riots and the gay liberation movement—Craig Rodwell, Frank Kameny, Marsha P. Johnson, Dick Leitsch, Thomas Lanigan-Schmidt, Brenda Howard, Rita Mae Brown, Sylvia Rivera, and many more. All of them used their voices, and organized, and agitated, and fought for what was right. That's what makes social change possible.

GAY LIBERATION,
CHRISTOPHER STREET PARK

Ten years after the Stonewall Inn, the gay liberation movement was well underway. Scores of gay organizations led marches and protests. They worked to change laws that allowed discrimination to occur against gay and lesbian people. And they created a gay subculture that was far more visible than the seedy Mafia-run bars of the 1960s. But there still was no public memorial of the Stonewall Riots, or any public art or monument honoring the gay liberation movement.

Bruce Voeller, the executive director of the National Gay Task Force (a group that was cofounded by Voeller and other members of the Gay Activists Alliance), had an idea. He approached a philanthropist named Peter Putnam, who ran a private arts foundation called the Mildred Andrews Fund, and asked him if he'd be willing to finance a Stonewall memorial. Putnam loved the idea, but he had some conditions. The artwork "had to be loving and caring, and show the affection that is the hallmark of gay people." It needed to represent women and men equally. And it needed to be installed on public land. Voeller accepted the terms, and the project was a go.

Getting the funding was the easy part. Everything else

about the project was challenging. First, there was finding an artist. Several gay and lesbian artists were approached to create the monument, but fearing public disclosure of their sexuality, they declined. Eventually, the commission chose George Segal, a heterosexual pop artist known for his public statues and monuments. The plan was for Segal to create two castings of a work titled *Gay Liberation*, and install one in New York City's Christopher Street Park, and the other in Los Angeles.

Segal created the figures for *Gay Liberation* using bronze casts made from plaster molds, then veneering the sculptures with a white finish. The final result is four figures—two standing males and two females seated on a park bench.

The next step was to get city approval. Although the project had support from political leaders, the *Village Voice*, and the director of historic parks, many Greenwich Village residents opposed the proposal. Some were offended by the subject matter and didn't like the fact that gay and lesbian people were taking over the neighborhood. Many of these residents were Irish and Italian Catholics whose families had lived in the area for generations. But there was some opposition from the gay and lesbian community, too, some of whom felt that a gay artist should have been chosen, others of whom thought the figures weren't representative of their community. All of this, coupled with a planned renovation of Christopher Street Park, delayed the project for years.

Meanwhile, the effort to install the second casting at a site in Los Angeles also hit some snags. The local government refused to accept the work, and after dealing with months of bureaucratic decision-making, it was ultimately installed on the Stanford University campus in Palo Alto, California. The sculpture was vandalized numerous times over the course of ten years, reminding people that even in the progressive San Francisco Bay Area, the fight for gay rights was far from over.

The casting that was initially intended for Sheridan Square in New York City was installed in a public park in Madison, Wisconsin, where it stayed from 1986 until 1991, with occasional removals for special gallery exhibits. In 1992, New York City officials finally agreed to install *Gay Liberation* in Christopher Street Park, in its rightful place across from the Stonewall Inn. The monument was officially unveiled by Mayor David Dinkins and Parks Commissioner Betsy Gotbaum on June 23, 1992.

Gay Liberation is a living conversation piece in Christopher Street Park. There is still lingering resentment from some gay and lesbian groups that a heterosexual artist was chosen for the project. Some think the gayness of the figures is too overt, while others think they're not overt enough. Some feel that the diversity of the LGBT community can't be captured in just four human figures. Some have raised concerns about the whiteness of the figures. In 2015, in protest of the whitewashing of Stonewall and the gay liberation movement, activists painted two of the figures' faces brown and accessorized them with wigs, bras, and scarves. *Gay Liberation* continues to inspire, to spark controversy, and to engage people in the fight for LGBT rights.

THE UNITED STATES STONEWALL NATIONAL MONUMENT SIGN

T he Greenwich Village Society for Historic Preservation, in collaboration with the Organization of Lesbian and Gay Architects and Designers, submitted a nomination for the Stonewall Inn, Christopher Street Park, and the neighboring streets to be added to the National Register of Historic Places. That designation was awarded on June 28, 1999, the first NRHP listing to be granted to a site with historical significance to the LGBT community. A few months later, on February 20, 2000, the same area was designated a National Historic Landmark. The Stonewall Inn became an official New York City Landmark on June 23, 2015, sparking interest from Greenwich Village residents to secure National Monument status for the Stonewall Inn and Christopher Street Park. The neighborhood community board, in partnership with the Greenwich Village Society for Historical Preservation, submitted a letter to the National Park Service requesting the designation. On June 24, 2016, President Barack Obama officially designated the Stonewall National Monument, making it the United States' first National Monument designated for an LGBT historic site. The area spans 7.7 acres, including Christopher

Street Park and the block of Christopher Street bordering the park, across the street from the Stonewall Inn.

Two weeks before the dedication ceremony, on June 12, a man named Omar Mateen committed a mass shooting at Pulse, a gay bar and nightclub in Orlando, Florida. Fifty people (including the shooter) died, and an additional fifty-three people were injured. At the time, it was the deadliest mass shooting by a single gunman in the United States. It is also the deadliest attack against the LGBT community in U.S. history. All of this gave the Stonewall National Monument dedication ceremony an even stronger meaning to the LGBT community.

THE STONEWALL INN TODAY

The Stonewall Inn, which was originally at 51 and 53 Christopher Street, closed in the fall of 1969, a few months after the riots occurred. Over the next two decades, various businesses occupied the space, including a bagel shop, a shoe store, and a Chinese restaurant. In the early 1990s, a bar called Stonewall opened at 53 Christopher Street.

The building was renovated in the late 1990s, and it reopened as a multi-floor nightclub. It stayed in operation until 2006, when it closed down due to noise complaints from neighbors, as well as general mismanagement. In 2007, three investors acquired the business, did a major renovation, and reopened the Stonewall Inn as a gay bar that March. It's been in operation ever since.

The inside of the modern Stonewall Inn is dark and dingy, and it can get hot and crowded. But it's matured since its Mafia days—it has a neon sign in the window, running water, and actual interior walls (as opposed to plywood). In many ways, it's just like many other gay bars, with drag shows, karaoke, and theme nights. But there's also no other place like it. The Stonewall Inn is where the gay community found its voice, seized its power, and took action. It's the birthplace of the modern LGBT rights movement—and once an entire community comes out of the closet, there's no turning back.

TIMELINE

1843 ★ Livery stable built at the site of 51 Christopher Street

1846 ★ Livery stable built at the site of 53 Christopher Street

FEBRUARY 21, 1903 ★ Police raid at the Ariston Baths, New York

FEBRUARY 16, 1918 ★ Police raid at the Baker Street Club, San
    Francisco

1930 ★ 51 and 53 Christopher Street reopens as Bonnie's Stone Wall

1950 ★ First meeting of the Mattachine Society

MAY 1953 ★ Founders of the Mattachine Society resign

OCTOBER 1955 ★ First meeting of the Daughters of Bilitis

MAY 1959 ★ Police raid at Cooper's Donuts

SEPTEMBER 14, 1961 ★ Police raid at the Tay-Bush Inn,
    San Francisco

APRIL 17, 1965 ★ First Mattachine Society picket (at the White
    House)

JULY 4, 1965 ★ First Annual Reminder picket at Independence
    Hall, Philadelphia

1966 ★ First meeting of PRIDE, Los Angeles
    ★ Bonnie's Stone Wall closes; Fat Tony purchases the
    property at 51 and 53 Christopher Street; site reopens as the
    Stonewall Inn

APRIL 21, 1966 ★ Sip-in at Julius' Bar, New York

AUGUST 1966 ★ Police raid at Gene Compton's Cafeteria,
    San Francisco

1967 ★ The CBS documentary *The Homosexuals* is aired

JANUARY 1, 1967 ★ Police raid at the Black Cat Tavern, Los Angeles

JUNE 22, 1969 ★ Judy Garland dies

JUNE 27, 1969 ★ Funeral held for Judy Garland

JUNE 28, 1969, EARLY MORNING ★ Police raid the Stonewall Inn
 ★ NYPD Tactical Patrol Force arrives
 ★ Howard Smith and Lucian Truscott IV from the *Village Voice* arrive on the scene
 ★ People barricaded inside the Stonewall Inn, including Dave Van Ronk, Seymour Pine, and *Village Voice* reporter Howard Smith
 ★ Parking meter used as a battering ram
 ★ Protestors form a kick line and resist the police
 ★ Four people arrested, including Dave Van Ronk and "the Stonewall Lesbian"
 ★ Craig Rodwell and Fred Sargeant arrive at the protest
 ★ Craig Rodwell leads "Gay Power!" chants
 ★ Volkswagen Beetle damaged
 ★ Marsha P. Johnson arrives at the protest (unclear)
 ★ Bob Kohler and Magoo arrive at the protest

DAYTIME ★ Craig Rodwell and Fred Sargeant distribute leaflets in Christopher Street Park and at the Oscar Wilde Memorial Bookshop
 ★ Dick Leitsch and a group of Mattachine Society members distribute an article titled "The Hairpin Drop Heard Around the World"
 ★ The Mattachine Society posts a sign on the Stonewall Inn

JUNE 28–29, 1969, LATE NIGHT/EARLY MORNING ★ A much larger crowd forms—second night of protesting

★ NYPD Tactical Patrol Force arrives

★ Protestors form a kick line and resist the police

★ Fred McDarrah photographs street kids outside the Stonewall Inn

★ Fred McDarrah photographs the inside of the Stonewall Inn

JUNE 29, 1969 ★ The *New York Times* publishes article about the raid

★ The New York *Daily News* publishes article

JUNE 29-30, 1969, LATE NIGHT/EARLY MORNING ★ Third night of protesting

★ NYPD Tactical Patrol Force arrives

★ Protestors form a kick line and resist the police

JUNE 30-JULY 1, 1969 ★ No protests (it was raining)

JULY 3, 1969 ★ The *Village Voice* publishes two articles about the riots: "Full Moon over the Stonewall" and "Gay Power Comes to Sheridan Square"

JULY 2-3, 1969, LATE NIGHT/EARLY MORNING ★ Protests against the *Village Voice*

★ NYPD Tactical Patrol Force arrives

★ Five people arrested, shops looted, many people injured

JULY 4, 1969 ★ Last Annual Reminder event at Independence Hall (two women held hands)

JULY 6, 1969 ★ New York *Daily News* publishes article "Homo Nest Raided, Queen Bees Are Stinging Mad"

JULY 9, 1969 ★ Gay Liberation Front forms

FALL 1969 ★ Stonewall Inn closes

NOVEMBER 2, 1969 ★ Resolution passed at the Eastern Regional Conference of Homophile Organizations (ERCHO) to hold annual demonstrations to commemorate the Stonewall Riots

DECEMBER 21, 1969 ★ Gay Activists Alliance forms

MARCH 8, 1970 ★ Police raid at the Snake Pit; Diego Viñales impaled by a fence spike

MAY 1, 1970 ★ Lavender Menace zap against NOW's Second Congress to Unite Women

JUNE 28, 1970 ★ First Christopher Street Liberation Day march held in New York
★ Gay dance held at NYU's Weinstein Hall

SEPTEMBER 1970 ★ Five-day sit-in held at NYU's Weinstein Hall

SEPTEMBER 25, 1970 ★ Unapproved gay dance held at NYU's Weinstein Hall
★ NYPD's Tactical Patrol Force arrives
★ Sylvia Rivera and others arrested

NOVEMBER 1970 ★ Sylvia Rivera and Marsha P. Johnson open STAR House

JULY 1971 ★ Residents of STAR House evicted

SEPTEMBER 1971 ★ NOW passes a resolution affirming lesbian rights

JUNE 24, 1973 ★ Sylvia Rivera makes "Y'all Better Quiet Down!" speech at the Christopher Street Liberation Day march

DECEMBER 11, 1973 ★ Mark Segal zaps *CBS Evening News with Walter Cronkite*

MAY 6, 1974 ★ Walter Cronkite airs news segment about gay rights

JUNE 23, 1992 ★ *Gay Liberation* sculpture unveiled in Christopher Street Park

JUNE 28, 1999 ★ The Stonewall Inn, Christopher Street Park, and neighboring streets added to the National Register of Historic Places

FEBRUARY 20, 2000 ★ The Stonewall Inn, Christopher Street Park, and neighboring streets designated a National Historic Landmark

2007 ★ The Stonewall Inn reopens as a gay bar

JUNE 23, 2015 ★ The Stonewall Inn designated an official New York City Landmark

JUNE 12, 2016 ★ Omar Mateen commits a mass shooting at the Pulse nightclub in Orlando, Florida

JUNE 24, 2016 ★ President Barack Obama designates the Stonewall National Monument

NOTES

OBJECT #1: JEFFERSON LIVERY STABLES

4   By the late 1800s . . . left on the streets to rot: Jennifer 8. Lee, "When Horses Posed a Public Health Hazard." *New York Times,* June 9, 2008; cityroom.blogs.nytimes. com/2008/06/09/when-horses-posed-a-public-health -hazard.

5   Saks & Company was one of the most elite . . . Saks's high-class image: Landmarks Preservation Commission, *Stonewall Inn.* New York, 2015; s-media.nyc.gov/agencies /lpc/lp/2574.pdf.

OBJECT #2: MATCHBOOK, BONNIE'S STONEWALL INN

7   The name Stone Wall . . . welcome message to lesbians: David Carter, *Stonewall: The Riots That Sparked the Gay Revolution.* New York: St. Martin's Press, 2004; page 8.

OBJECT #3: TRIAL TRANSCRIPT, JUNE 8, 1903

10   One attorney showed . . . he was heterosexual: *People of the State of New York v. Michael Schnittel* (Trial 355), 1903 Court of General Sessions (1903).

10   Another called a series . . . heterosexual man: *People of the State of New York v. Walter Bennett* (Trial 369), 1903 Court of General Sessions (1903).

10   Still another argued . . . during his arrest: Brian Donovan, *Respectability on Trial: Sex Crimes in New York City, 1900–1918.* New York: SUNY Press, 2016; page 158.

11   The message was clear . . . jailed for it: Bill Lipsky, "The Fabulous Baker Street Boys." *San Francisco Bay Times,* sfbaytimes.com/the-fabulous-baker-street-boys.

OBJECT #4: 1950s TELEVISION

14 During commercial breaks . . . in front of the television: Betty
    Friedan, *The Feminine Mystique*. New York: W. W. Norton, 1963;
    pages 15–16.

14 On top of that . . . what kind could not: Motion Picture
    Association of America, Production Code Administration
    records, Margaret Herrick Library, Academy of Motion
    Picture Arts and Sciences.

OBJECT #9: "GAY IS GOOD" BUTTON

29 As a result, throughout the early twentieth century . . . better
    than black people: Ibram X. Kendi, *Stamped from the Beginning:
    The Definitive History of Racist Ideas in America*. New York:
    Nation Books, 2016; page 343.

30 "A CBS poll shows . . . disgust, discomfort, or fear": Mike
    Wallace, William Peters, and Harry Morgan, *The
    Homosexuals: CBS Reports*. New York: CBS Television,
    March 7, 1967.

OBJECT #13: PHOTOGRAPH, SIP-IN AT JULIUS' BAR

43 "We are homosexuals . . . we are orderly": Jim Farber, "Before
    the Stonewall Uprising, There was the 'Sip-In," *New York Times*,
    April 20, 2016. See www.nytimes.com/2016/04/21/nyregion/
    before-the-stonewall-riots-there-was-the-sip-in.html.

OBJECT #15: DOROTHY'S DRESS, *THE WIZARD OF OZ*

50 "You could actually feel it in the air. You really could":
    "Stonewall Riots 40th Anniversary: A Look Back at the
    Uprising That Launched the Modern Gay Rights Movement."
    Democracy Now. Arlington, PA: PBS Television, June 26, 2009;
    www.democracynow.org/2009/6/26/stonewall_riots_40th_
    anniversary_a_look.

OBJECT #16: NYPD OFFICIAL POLICE HAT, CIRCA 1960S

57 The Sixth Precinct . . . but raids happened anyway: Carter, *Stonewall*; pages 79, 82.

59 Eventually, two police wagons . . . inside to exit the building: Lincoln Anderson, "'I'm Sorry,' Says Inspector Who Led Stonewall Raid." *Villager*, vol. 73, no. 7, June 16–22, 2004; thevillager.com/villager_59/imsorrysaysinspector.html.

59 "If what I did helped gay people, then I'm glad": Dennis Hevesi, "Seymour Pine Dies at 91; Led Raid on Stonewall Inn." *New York Times*, Sept. 7, 2010; www.nytimes.com/2010/09/08 /nyregion/08pine.html.

OBJECT #17: NYPD-ISSUED NIGHTSTICK, CIRCA 1960S

61 As you might imagine . . . and even death: PoliceOne Staff, "History and Use of the Billy Club." PoliceOne, Nov. 16, 2016; www.policeone.com/police-history/articles/241403006 -History-and-use-of-the-billy-club.

OBJECT #18: PHOTOGRAPH, STORMÉ DELARVERIE

64 Stormé was in New York . . . She says she was: Susan SurfTone, "The Night I Met Stormé DeLarverie, the Lesbian Who Threw the First Punch at Stonewall." AfterEllen, May 2, 2018; www.afterellen.com/people/558507-the-night-i-met -storme-delarverie-the-lesbian-who-threw-the-first-punch -at-stonewall.

66 So do others . . . Charles Kaiser: Charles Kaiser, *The Gay Metropolis: 1940–1996*. New York: Houghton Mifflin, 1997; page 198.

66 Stormé herself didn't . . . thirty-nine years after Stonewall: Patrick Hinds, "Uncovering the Stonewall Lesbian: Stormé DeLarverie Was There That Infamous Night. Now She's Coming Clean About It All." *Curve Magazine*, Jan. 1, 2008.

66　In fact, at least . . . instantly recognizable: Candice Frederick, "LGBT Icon Stormé DeLarverie's Personal Collection Comes to the Schomburg." New York Public Library, June 23, 2017; www. nypl.org/blog/2017/06/23/lgbt-icon-storme.

66　"I sprung up . . . of the Stonewall": Leslie Feinberg, "Stonewall Rebellion: Crowd Rage Ignites." *Workers World*, June 15, 2006; www.workers.org/2006/us/lavender-red-66.

67　"not really feminine or masculine": Jonathan Ned Katz, "'I didn't know I was going to be part of history': Jonathan Ned Katz Interviews Raymond Castro." *OutHistory*, June 16, 2009; outhistory.org/exhibits/show/stonewall-riot-police-reports /contents/interview-raymond-castro.

OBJECT #19: PHOTOGRAPH, CRAIG RODWELL INSIDE THE ORIGINAL OSCAR WILDE MEMORIAL BOOKSHOP

69　"All of a sudden . . . 'Gay Power!'": Soterios Johnson, "Stonewall Remembered." WNYC/New York Public Radio, New York City, July 2, 2016; www.wnyc.org/story/stonewall-remembered.

72　The Oscar Wilde . . . closed its doors permanently: Craig Rodwell, "Craig Rodwell Papers, 1940–1993." New York Public Library Manuscripts and Archives Division; www.nypl.org/sites/default/files/archivalcollections/pdf/ rodwell.pdf.

OBJECT #20: ARREST RECORD, DAVE VAN RONK

74　"I was passing . . . riot without me!": Tony Russell, "Dave Van Ronk: Musician and Mentor to the Young Bob Dylan." *Guardian*, Feb. 12, 2002; www.theguardian.com/news/2002 /feb/13/guardianobituaries.

75　"Pine, a man . . . him for assault'": Howard Smith, "Full Moon Over Stonewall," *Village Voice*, vol. XIV, no. 28; July 3, 1969.

OBJECT #21: PHOTOGRAPH, 1968 VOLKSWAGEN BEETLE

80 By the late 1960s . . . a hippie car: Bernhard Reiger, *The People's Car: A Global History of the Volkswagen Beetle*. Cambridge, MA: Harvard University Press, 2013; pages 213, 218–219.

80 One of them . . . identity is unknown: "Report 6: Complaint (Volkswagen Owner)." New York, 1969; www.outhistory.org /exhibits/show/stonewall-riot-police-reports/contents/report-6.

OBJECT #23: NEW YORK CITY PARKING METER, CIRCA 1960S

86 Some witnesses remember . . . meter was uprooted: Carter, *Stonewall*; page 165.

OBJECT #25: PHOTOGRAPH, MAGOO, BOB KOHLER'S DOG

91 Things quickly got out of control . . . amid the chaos: Carter, *Stonewall*; page 167.

91 "I'm just taking my dog out for a walk": Fred Sargeant, interviewed by the author via email communication, March 22, 2015.

92 After Magoo died . . . his beloved dog: Janet Kwon, "At 80, Activist Recalls a Lifetime on the Front Lines," *Villager*, vol. 76, no. 5, June 21–27, 2006; thevillager.com/villager_164 /at80activistrecalls.html.

OBJECT #26: VIEW FROM THE THIRD-FLOOR FIRE ESCAPE AT 84 GROVE STREET

94 "There weren't a lot of people . . . were horribly mistreated": Margot Avery, interviewed by the author via phone, June 20, 2018.

OBJECT #27: PHOTOGRAPH, PROTESTORS OUTSIDE THE STONEWALL INN

97 McDarrah and his colleague . . . the Stonewall Inn: Lucian K. Truscott IV, "The Real Mob at Stonewall," *New York Times*, June 25, 2009; www.nytimes.com/2009/06/26 /opinion/26truscott.html.

97 "They said something . . . 'you're *like that*'": Thomas Lanigan-
Schmidt, "Thomas Lanigan-Schmidt by Jessica Baran,"
interview by Jessica Baran. *Bomb Magazine*, April 16, 2013;
bombmagazine.org/articles/thomas-lanigan-schmidt.

99 "The place wasn't glamorous . . . smell going through it":
Thomas Lanigan-Schmidt, "Tommy Lanigan-Schmidt, One
of the Last Surviving Stonewall Street Youths, Reviews the
Movie," interview by James St. James. World of Wonder, Sept.
25, 2015; worldofwonder.net/tommy-lanigan-schmidt-one-of-
the-last-surviving-stonewall-street-youths-reviews-the-movie.

100 Twenty years after . . . June 28, 1969: Thomas Lanigan-
Schmidt, "1969 Mother Stonewall and the Golden Rats";
myqueertestimony.tumblr.com/post/44555514250/1969
-mother-stonewall-and-the-golden-rats-1989.

100 "No, this wasn't . . . That's all": Ibid.

OBJECT #29: LEAFLET DISTRIBUTED BY CRAIG RODWELL

105 "Getting coverage . . . means of communication": Fred Sargeant,
"Anger Management." *New York Times*, June 25, 2009; www.
nytimes.com/2009/06/26/opinion/26sargeant.html.

OBJECT #33: *VILLAGE VOICE* ARTICLE, "FULL MOON OVER THE STONEWALL" AND OBJECT #34: *VILLAGE VOICE* ARTICLE, "GAY POWER COMES TO SHERIDAN SQUARE"

111 "I saw about thirty people . . . raced downstairs": Johnson,
"Stonewall Remembered."

112 "All it ever took . . . they resisted": Soterios Johnson,
"Stonewall Remembered."

112 "The cops had . . . in the crowd" Howard Smith, "Full Moon
Over Stonewall," *Village Voice*, vol. XIV, no. 28; July 3, 1969.

114 "I was on Christopher . . . freaks easily": Johnson, "Stonewall
Remembered."

114 "People started pulling . . . letting it all out, finally": Johnson, "Stonewall Remembered."

115 "The thumping . . . went crazy": Johnson, "Stonewall Remembered."

116 "Gay Power! . . . possibility, and pride": Lucian Truscott IV, "Gay Power Comes to Sheridan Square," *Village Voice*, July 3, 1969; www.columbia.edu/cu/lweb/eresources/exhibitions/sw25/voice_19690703_truscott.html.

OBJECT #36: NEW YORK *DAILY NEWS* ARTICLE, "HOMO NEST RAIDED, QUEEN BEES ARE STINGING MAD"

121 "Last weekend the queens . . . carnivorous jungle plants": Jerry Lisker, "Homo Nest Raided, Queen Bees Are Stinging Mad," New York *Daily News*, July 6, 1969.

OBJECT #38: GAY ACTIVISTS ALLIANCE (GAA) POLITICAL PATCH

129 The zap . . . news segment about gay rights: Mark Segel, *And Then I Danced*. Brooklyn, NY: Akashic Books, 2015; pages 80–91.

OBJECT #39: ORNAMENTAL IRON FENCE, GREENWICH VILLAGE, NEW YORK CITY

133 By this time . . . against their community: NYC LGBT Historic Sites Project, "The Snake Pit." NYC LGBT Historic Sites Project, www.nyclgbtsites.org/site/the-snake-pit.

OBJECT #40: RITA MAE BROWN'S LAVENDER MENACE T-SHIRT

136 "You're Going . . . *IS* a Lesbian Plot": Rita Mae Brown, *Rita Will: Memoir of a Literary Rabble-Rouser*. New York: Bantam Books, 1997; pages 223, 232–236.

136 "Finally, we were ready . . . The audience was on our side": Karla Jay, *Tales of the Lavender Menace: A Memoir of Liberation*. New York: Basic Books, 1999; page 143.

OBJECT #41: CHRISTOPHER STREET LIBERATION DAY MARCH ADVERTISEMENT

139 "That the Annual Reminder . . . a nationwide show of support": Craig Rodwell, "Gay Holiday," Hymnal 2, no. 1, January 1970, page 8. Quoted in David Carter, *Stonewall: The Riots That Sparked the Gay Revolution*. New York: St. Martin's Press, 2004; page 230.

140 Howard solicited . . . Oscar Wilde Memorial Bookshop: Fred Sargeant, interviewed by the author via email communication, March 22, 2015. Fundraising flyers and accounting logs, Foster Gunnison Papers, University of Connecticut Special Collections, Box 9, folders 80–83, accessed June 20, 2015. Lillian Faderman, *The Gay Revolution: The Story of the Struggle* (New York: Simon & Schuster, 2015), pages 198–199.

OBJECT #42: PHOTOGRAPH, BRENDA HOWARD WITH PROTEST SIGN

143 "in-your-face" . . . "rights trampled on": Eliel Cruz, "Remembering Brenda: An Ode to the 'Mother of Pride.'" *Advocate*, June 17, 2014; www.advocate.com/bisexuality/2014/06/17/remembering-brenda-ode-%E2%80%98mother-pride%E2%80%99.

OBJECT #43: MAP OF THE CHRISTOPHER STREET LIBERATION DAY MARCH ROUTE

146 This map details . . . Liberation Day march: Foster Gunnison Papers, University of Connecticut Special Collections, Box 53, Folder 617, accessed June 10, 2015.

OBJECT #46: STREET TRANSVESTITE ACTION REVOLUTIONARIES BANNER

151 "morally acceptable": Martin Duberman, *Stonewall*. New York: Dutton, 1993; page 314.

153 "STAR was for . . . control at the bars": Leslie Feinberg, "Street Transvestite Action Revolutionaries: Lavender & Red, part 73." *Workers World*, Sept. 24, 2006; www.workers.org/2006/us/lavender-red-73.

OBJECT #47: SYLVIA RIVERA AT THE 1973 CHRISTOPHER STREET LIBERATION DAY MARCH

154 Sylvia Rivera, "Y'all Better Quiet Down," Archive .org video, 4:08, 1973. See archive.org/details/SylviaRiveraYallBetterQuietDown1973.

OBJECT #48: *GAY LIBERATION*, CHRISTOPHER STREET PARK

164 The monument was . . . June 23, 1992: NYC Parks, "Christopher Park: Gay Liberation." NYC Parks; www.nycgovparks.org/parks/christopher-park/monuments/575.

165 In 2015, in protest . . . wigs, bras, and scarves: Bil Browning, "Vandals Paint Stonewall Statues to Protest 'Whitewashing.'" *Advocate*, Aug. 19, 2015; www.advocate.com/stonewall/2015/08/19/activists-vandalize-new-york-city-stonewall-monument-protest-whitewashing.

BIBLIOGRAPHY

PRIMARY SOURCES

Foster Gunnison Papers (fundraising flyers and accounting logs).
University of Connecticut Special Collections, Box 53, Folder
617. Accessed June 10, 2015.

Landmarks Preservation Commission. *Stonewall Inn.*
New York, 2015. See s-media.nyc.gov/agencies/lpc/
lp/2574.pdf.

People of the State of New York v. Michael Schnittel (Trial 355), 1903
Court of General Sessions (1903).

People of the State of New York v. Walter Bennett (Trial 369), 1903
Court of General Sessions (1903).

"Report 6: Complaint (Volkswagen Owner)." New York, 1969.
See www.outhistory.org/exhibits/show/stonewall-riot
-police-reports/contents/report-6.

Rivera, Sylvia. "Y'all Better Quiet Down." Archive.org
video, 4:08. 1873. See https://archive.org/details/
SylviaRiveraYallBetterQuietDown1973.

Sargeant, Fred. Interviewed by the author via email
communication: In 2015, March 18, 20, 22, 29; April 16; May
29; June 20; September 7, 12. In 2018, July 11.

BOOKS

Brown, Rita Mae. *Rita Will: Memoir of a Literary Rabble-Rouser.*
New York: Bantam Books, 1997.

Carter, David. *Stonewall: The Riots That Sparked the Gay Revolution.*
New York: St. Martin's Press, 2004.

Donovan, Brian. *Respectability on Trial: Sex Crimes in New York City,
1900–1918.* New York: SUNY Press, 2016.

Duberman, Martin. *Stonewall.* New York: Dutton, 1993.

Faderman, Lillian. *The Gay Revolution: The Story of the Struggle.* New York: Simon & Schuster, 2015.

Friedan, Betty. *The Feminine Mystique.* New York: W. W. Norton, 1963.

Jay, Karla. *Tales of the Lavender Menace: A Memoir of Liberation.* New York: Basic Books, 1999.

Kaiser, Charles. *The Gay Metropolis: 1940–1996.* New York: Houghton Mifflin, 1997.

Kendi, Ibram X. *Stamped from the Beginning: The Definitive History of Racist Ideas in America.* New York: Nation Books, 2016.

Reiger, Bernhard. *The People's Car: A Global History of the Volkswagen Beetle.* Cambridge, MA: Harvard University Press, 2013.

Segal, Mark. *And Then I Danced: Traveling the Road to LGBT Equality.* Brooklyn, NY: Akashic Books, 2015.

ARTICLES, PAPERS, AND WEBSITES

Anderson, Lincoln. "'I'm Sorry,' Says Inspector Who Led Stonewall Raid." *Villager,* vol. 73, no. 7, June 16–22, 2004; thevillager.com/villager_59/imsorrysaysinspector.html.

Browning, Bil. "Vandals Paint Stonewall Statues to Protest 'Whitewashing.'" *Advocate,* Aug. 19, 2015; www.advocate.com/stonewall/2015/08/19/activists-vandalize-new-york-city-stonewall-monument-protest-whitewashing.

Cruz, Eliel. "Remembering Brenda: An Ode to the 'Mother of Pride.'" *Advocate,* June 17, 2014; www.advocate.com/bisexuality/2014/06/17/remembering-brenda-ode-%E2%80%98mother-pride%E2%80%99.

Faber, Jim. "Before the Stonewall Uprising, There was the 'Sip-In.'" *New York Times.* April 20, 2016. See www.nytimes.com/2016/04/21/nyregion/before-the-stonewall-riots-there-was-the-sip-in.html.

Feinberg, Leslie. "Stonewall Rebellion: Crowd Rage Ignites." *Workers World,* June 15, 2006; www.workers.org/2006/us /lavender-red-66.

Feinberg, Leslie. "Street Transvestite Action Revolutionaries: Lavender & Red, part 73." *Workers World*, Sept. 24, 2006; www.workers.org/2006/us/lavender-red-73.

Frederick, Candice. "LGBT Icon Stormé DeLarverie's Personal Collection Comes to the Schomburg." New York Public Library, June 23, 2017; www.nypl.org/blog/2017/06/23/lgbt -icon-storme.

Hevesi, Dennis. "Seymour Pine Dies at 91; Led Raid on Stonewall Inn." *New York Times*, Sept. 7, 2010; www.nytimes .com/2010/09/08/nyregion/08pine.html.

Hinds, Patrick. "Uncovering the Stonewall Lesbian: Stormé DeLarverie Was There That Infamous Night. Now She's Coming Clean About It All." *Curve Magazine*, Jan. 1, 2008.

Katz, Jonathan Ned. "'I Didn't Know I Was Going to Be Part of History': Jonathan Ned Katz Interviews Raymond Castro." *OutHistory*, June 16, 2009; outhistory.org/exhibits/ show/stonewall-riot-police-reports/contents/interview- raymond-castro.

Kwon, Janet. "At 80, Activist Recalls a Lifetime on the Front Lines." *Villager*, vol. 76, no. 5, June 21–27, 2006; thevillager.com/villager_164/at80activistrecalls.html.

Lanigan-Schmidt, Thomas. "1969 Mother Stonewall and the Golden Rats." See myqueertestimony.tumblr.com /post/44555514250/1969-mother-stonewall-and-the-golden -rats-1989.

Lanigan-Schmidt, Thomas. "Thomas Lanigan-Schmidt by Jessica Baran." Interview by Jessica Baran. *Bomb Magazine*, April 16, 2013; bombmagazine.org/articles/thomas-lanigan- schmidt.

Lanigan-Schmidt, Thomas. "Tommy Lanigan-Schmidt, One of
the Last Surviving Stonewall Street Youths, Reviews the
Movie." Interview by James St. James. *World of Wonder*,
Sept. 25, 2015; worldofwonder.net/tommy-lanigan-schmidt-
one-of-the-last-surviving-stonewall-street-youths-reviews-
the-movie.

Lee, Jennifer 8. "When Horses Posed a Public Health Hazard."
New York Times, June 9, 2008; cityroom.blogs.nytimes
.com/2008/06/09/when-horses-posed-a-public-health-
hazard.

Lipsky, Bill. "The Fabulous Baker Street Boys." *San Francisco
Bay Times*. See sfbaytimes.com/the-fabulous-baker-street-
boys.

Lisker, Jerry. "Homo Nest Raided, Queen Bees Are Stinging
Mad." New York *Daily News*. July 6, 1969.

NYC LGBT Historic Sites Project. "The Snake Pit." NYC
LGBT Historic Sites Project; www.nyclgbtsites.org/site
/the-snake-pit.

NYC Parks, "Christopher Park: Gay Liberation." NYC Parks;
www.nycgovparks.org/parks/christopher-park
/monuments/575.

PoliceOne Staff. "History and Use of the Billy Club." PoliceOne,
Nov. 16, 2016; www.policeone.com/police-history
/articles/241403006-History-and-use-of-the-billy-club.

Rodwell, Craig. "Craig Rodwell Papers, 1940–1993." New York
Public Library Manuscripts and Archives Division.
Compiled by Laura K. O'Keefe, June 1995. See www.nypl.org
/sites/default/files/archivalcollections/pdf/rodwell.pdf.

Russell, Tony. "Dave Van Ronk: Musician and Mentor to the
Young Bob Dylan." *Guardian,* Feb. 12, 2002; www
.theguardian.com/news/2002/feb/13/guardianobituaries.

Sargeant, Fred. "Anger Management." *New York Times*, June 25,

2009; www.nytimes.com/2009/06/26/opinion/26sargeant
.html.

Smith, Howard. "Full Moon Over Stonewall." *Village Voice*, vol.
XIV, no. 28; July 3, 1969.

SurfTone, Susan. "The Night I Met Stormé DeLarverie, the
Lesbian Who Threw the First Punch at Stonewall."
AfterEllen, May 2, 2018; www.afterellen.com/people/558507
-the-night-i-met-storme-delarverie-the-lesbian-who-threw
-the-first-punch-at-stonewall.

Truscott, Lucian IV. "Gay Power Comes to Sheridan Square."
Village Voice, July 3, 1969; www.columbia.edu/cu/lweb
/eresources/exhibitions/sw25/voice_19690703_truscott.html.

Truscott, Lucian K. IV. "The Real Mob at Stonewall." *New York
Times*, June 25, 2009; www.nytimes.com/2009/06/26
/opinion/26truscott.html.

BROADCAST, RADIO, AND TV

Johnson, Soterios. "Stonewall Remembered." WNYC/New York
Public Radio. New York: July 2, 2016; www.wnyc.org/story
/stonewall-remembered.

"Stonewall Riots 40th Anniversary: A Look Back at the Uprising
That Launched the Modern Gay Rights Movement."
Democracy Now. Arlington, PA: PBS Television, June 26,
2009; www.democracynow.org/2009/6/26/stonewall
_riots_40th_anniversary_a_look.

Wallace, Mike, William Peters, and Harry Morgan, *The
Homosexuals*, *CBS Reports*. New York, NY, CBS Television,
March 7, 1967.

ACKNOWLEDGMENTS

R evolutions aren't launched by a single person. In fact, some of the most effective activists are those who work behind the scenes. The same is true when it comes to writing a book, and I'd like to take the opportunity to thank all of you who helped me tell the Stonewall story.

Librarians are some of the greatest people on earth, and those who work in special collections were particularly helpful to me as I researched this book. I'd like to thank Jason Baumann, Coordinator of Humanities and LGBT Collections at the New York Public Library; all of the staff at the New York Public Library Schomburg Center for Research in Black Culture; Kristin Eshelman and Graham Stinnett at the University of Connecticut Library; Jeremy Prince, director and curator at the GLBT Historical Society; the staff at the ONE National Gay & Lesbian Archives at the University of Southern California; the librarians and archivists at the James C. Hormel LGBTQIA Center at the San Francisco Public Library; and the staff at the New York Historical Society. The archival materials housed at these institutions were invaluable in the creation of this book.

Archival material is helpful, but nothing is more valuable than hearing first-person accounts. I am especially grateful to Fred Sargeant, who helped me get as close as possible to the "truth" of what happened the night the Stonewall Inn was raided. Without your guidance, generosity of time and energy, and friendship, this book would never have come to life. Thanks to Margot Avery for providing a glimpse of the Stonewall Riots from a ten-year-old's perspective, and to Ellen Broidy for helping me fill in some informational gaps. Susan Iger and Lisa Beth Kovetz at CUNY TV were instrumental in helping me connect with some of these individuals, and I'm grateful to you both.

I'm not a detail person at all, and so I have a deep appreciation for those who are. Thanks to Natalie Tomiyoshi for digging deep into archival materials, for your meticulous documentation, and for going back and forth from Harlem to lower Manhattan to photograph various items. A special thanks to Mark Vieira for coming to my rescue at the final hour to nail down all the fine-grained details necessary for a work of nonfiction.

Writing can be a lonely and solitary endeavor, and I can't imagine doing it without my writing community. I'd like to thank my fellow children's book writers and illustrators, including JaNay Brown-Wood, Erin Dealey, Alex Gino, Maya Gonzalez, Mike Jung, Patricia Newman, Joanna Rowland, and Nikki Shannon Smith. A special thanks to Jen Barton and Elizabeth Siggins for reading and critiquing various drafts of this book, for our productive and therapeutic writing retreats, and for being my friends. Thanks to Lee Wind, for blogging, signal-boosting, and uplifting queer writing voices in general; to Cathy Renna, for your friendship and your savvy knowledge of LGBTQ+ journalism and media; and to Emma Dryden, for your grounded advice and unwavering support of my writing career. Thanks to Deborah Warren and the team at East/West Literary Agency. Deborah, you have a heart of gold, and I appreciate the depths you've been willing to go to support me. A special thanks to my editor Howard Reeves, editorial assistant Emily Daluga, managing editor Amy Vreeland, art director Pam Notarantonio, designers Steph Stilwell and Sara Corbett, and the rest of the team at Abrams. I know it's not easy to work with an author who's finishing a book while working full-time and trying to be a decent parent, and I can't tell you how much I appreciate your patience. Lastly, I want to thank Lesléa Newman for your friendship, mentorship, and networking. You're the reason this book shifted from a mere idea to a reality.

Thanks to all of my students and colleagues at Sacramento City College, who have been incredibly supportive and encouraging throughout this project. A special thanks to Bill Doonan, whose book *A History of Sacramento City College in 100 Objects* gave me the idea for the format of this book.

Amy and Rowan, I love you both more than anything. Thank you for giving me the time and space to do this work.

Lastly, thanks to all of the brave LGBTQ+ activists who stood up, raised their voices, and fought back. You inspire me every day to do the same.

IMAGE CREDITS

Page 5: Jessie Tarbox Beals/Museum of the City of New York (96.127.17). **Page 6:** From Gayle E. Pitman's personal collection. **Page 13:** ClassicStock/Alamy Stock Photo. **Page 16:** San Francisco History Center, San Francisco Public Library. **Page 20:** ONE Archives at the USC Libraries. **Page 23:** ONE Archives at the USC Libraries. **Page 25:** Photo by Kay Tobin, © Manuscripts and Archives Division, The New York Public Library. **Page 28:** ONE Archives at the USC Libraries. **Page 31:** Photo by Nancy Tucker, courtesy Lesbian Herstory Archives via ONE Archives at the USC Libraries. **Page 33:** From Gayle E. Pitman's personal collection. **Page 39:** ONE Archives at the USC Libraries. **Pages 44–45:** Fred W. McDarrah/Getty Images. **Page 52:** iStock.com/blackwaterimages. **Page 57:** From Gayle E. Pitman's personal collection. **Page 60:** From Gayle E. Pitman's personal collection. **Page 69:** Photo by Kay Tobin, © Manuscripts and Archives Division, The New York Public Library. **Page 79:** From Gayle E. Pitman's personal collection. **Page 83:** ONE Archives at the USC Libraries. **Page 85:** From Gayle E. Pitman's personal collection. **Page 89:** NBC/Getty Images. **Page 93:** From Gayle E. Pitman's personal collection. **Page 98:** Fred W. McDarrah/Getty Images. **Page 101:** Fred W. McDarrah/Getty Images. **Page 105:** From Fred Sargeant's personal collection. **Page 107:** June 29, 1969, p. 33, *The New York Times* Archives. **Page 108:** Fred W. McDarrah/Getty Images. **Page 110:** Fred W. McDarrah/Getty Images. **Page 120:** Photo by Nancy Tucker, courtesy Lesbian Herstory Archives via ONE Archives at the

USC Libraries. **Page 122:** From Gayle E. Pitman's personal collection. **Page 127:** From Gayle E. Pitman's personal collection. **Page 131:** iStock.com/JayLazarin. **Page 135:** Photo by Diana Davies, © Manuscripts and Archives Division, The New York Public Library. **Page 141:** From Fred Sargeant's personal collection. **Pages 144–145:** Richard C. Wandel Photographs, Lesbian, Gay, Bisexual & Transgender Community Center Archives, New York City. **Page 147:** Foster Gunnison Jr. Papers, Archives and Special Collections at the Thomas J. Dodd Research Center, University of Connecticut Library. **Page 148:** From Gayle E. Pitman's personal collection. **Page 150:** Richard C. Wandel Photographs Collection. **Page 155:** ONE Archives at the USC Libraries. **Page 165:** Courtesy Sidney Janis Gallery, New York, via ONE Archives at the USC Libraries. **Page 167:** iStock.com/Joel Carillet. **Page 168:** iStock.com/mizoula.

Back Cover: Photo by Nancy Tucker, courtesy Lesbian Herstory Archives via ONE Archives at the USC Libraries.

INDEX

Note: Page numbers in *italics* refer to illustrations.